THE CLANS
& TARTANS OF
SCOTLAND

ABOVE: Caerlaverock Castle, in Dumfries & Galloway, was the stronghold of Clan Maxwell from the 13th–17th centuries after which it was abandoned.

OPPOSITE: The impressive red deer is Britain's largest terrestrial mammal and Scotland's most iconic species.

THE CLANS
& TARTANS OF
SCOTLAND

Contributing Editor: Peter B. Stuart

CHARTWELL
BOOKS

This edition published in 2015 by
CHARTWELL BOOKS
an imprint of Book Sales
a division of Quarto Publishing Group USA Inc.
142 West 36th Street, 4th Floor
New York, NY 10018
USA

Copyright © 2015
Regency House Publishing Limited
The Manor House
High Street
Buntingford
Hertfordshire
SG9 9AB
United Kingdom

For all editorial enquiries, please contact
www.regencyhousepublishing.com

All rights reserved. No part of this book may be reproduced in
any form or by any electronic or mechanical means, including
information, storage and retrieval systems, without permission in
writing from the copyright holder.

ISBN-13: 978-0-7858-3285-0

Printed in China

The text in this title, *The Clans and Tartans of Scotland,* was
originally published by Regency House Publishing Limited as
Clans and Tartans of Scotland by Neil Grant.

The author and the publisher cannot accept any legal
responsibility for omissions and errors in this book.

*Urquhart Castle, overlooking Loch Ness, was a royal seat before it was given to Clan
Grant in 1509.*

CONTENTS

INTRODUCTION

The origins of the clans are varied: some were of Pictish descent, some Norse, and some sprang from the early settlers in Dalriada. The great Clan Donald, a name which in its original Gaelic version means 'ruler of the world', was descended from Somerled, a formidable 12th-century chieftain who, notwithstanding his Norse name, could trace his own ancestry to the High Kings of Ireland. He acquired a large dominion in Argyll and the Western Isles, and the various branches of Clan Donald stemmed from his sons. In the east and north, many clan chiefs were descended from feudal Anglo-Norman landlords whose men adopted their names when surnames came into use in the Highlands towards the end of the Middle Ages.

Clan names generally derived from some semi-mythical figure from a much earlier age than that of the historical founder, such as Somerled, who acquired the land that gave them their existence. (As in Ireland, the old Celtic genealogies cannot always be taken on trust, though where they can be checked against other evidence they often turn out to be more reliable than might be expected.) The Campbells are called Clan Diarmaid, after an

Eilean Mór, Loch Finlaggan, seat of the Lord of the Isles and the Clan MacDonald. Finlaggan Castle, also known as Eilean Mór Castle, is now a ruin.

ancient hero forever lost in the mists of Celtic antiquity, but the Campbell chief (the Duke of Argyll) is called *Mac Cailein Mór*, 'Son of Great Colin', after Sir Colin Campbell, knighted by King Alexander III in 1280, a substantial figure whose own ancestors can be traced back, with reasonable confidence, for at least six generations.

Lands were generally built up gradually over time, not only by conquest but also by marriage, royal grant or other means. But, whatever the legal title, land had to be held by force, and clan chiefs were therefore eager to acquire men as well as land.

Castle Campbell is a medieval castle situated above the town of Dollar, Clackmannanshire, in central Scotland. It was the lowland seat of the earls and dukes of Argyll, chiefs of Clan Campbell from the 15th to the 19th centuries, and was visited by Mary, Queen of Scots, in the 16th century.

The military aspect of the clan system, combined with devotion to the clan homeland, reinforced the powerful spirit of clanship. Because the men of the clan believed that they and their chief were of the same kin, a much stronger bond existed between chief and clansman than between landlord and feudal tenant. Of course there were social distinctions, but there was also mutual respect and a refreshing lack of lordly superiority or servile humility from either one. English visitors in the 18th century were surprised to observe that a great clan chief would talk to his herdsmen and labourer on terms of equality.

Clans were numerous and varied: while some prospered and expanded, others declined and disappeared. Large clans developed many branches, septs and dependants, including other, lesser clans that settled on their land. Members did not necessarily even share the same name, and if they did it might have been recently adopted for convenience and, in the event of a change of allegiance, might be changed again. The extent to which they could be regarded as true clans also varied. Some, like the Gordons, were merely the tenantry of a powerful family, held together by feudal loyalties rather than kinship.

The clan system was essentially a Highland

development, but was also characteristic of the Borders. In both regions, clan loyalties were cemented by constant conflicts, over land, cattle or other objectives, and by the ferocious, lengthy blood feuds that they provoked. In greater conflicts, such as civil wars, different clans fought on different sides and were motivated as much by clan hatreds as by political or religious animosities.

During the Jacobite revolt of 1715, MacLean of Duart addressed his men at Sheriffmuir: 'Gentlemen, this is a day we have long wished to see. Yonder stands Mac Cailean Mór [i.e. Campbell] for King George. Here stands Maclean for King James. God bless MacLean and King James! Gentlemen, charge!'

Duart Castle, on the Isle of Mull, off the west coast of Scotland. The castle dates back to the 13th century and is the seat of Clan MacLean.

Agnew ancient

AGNEW

Motto: *Consilio non impetu* (By wisdom not by force).

War Cry: '*Agnew*'.

Heraldic Badge: An eagle looking back over its shoulder.

Origin of Name: The origin of the name Agnew is disputed though it is generally thought to be Norman, from the Barony d'Agneaux. A separate origin has also been suggested through the Celtic natives of Ulster, the O'Gnimh, who were the hereditary poets or bards of the O'Neills of Clanaboy, who acquired the anglicized name Agnew.

Origin of Clan: The fortunes of the Agnew clan were established in Scotland in 1426 when Andrew of Lochnaw was granted the constableship and lands of Lochnaw Castle. In 1451 he was appointed Sheriff of Wigtown, an hereditary title passed down through generations, and his direct descendants still hold office today.

Lands: Dumfriesshire, Galloway.

Associated Castle: Lochnaw Castle, Dumfries & Galloway.

ANDERSON

Anderson ancient

Motto: Stand sure.

Heraldic Badge: An oak tree.

Plant: Oak tree.

Origin of Name: St. Andrew is patron saint of Scotland, and the surname Anderson, which literally means 'Son of Andrew', is found over most of the country. The Gaelic derivation of the name is *Gilleaindreas* meaning 'Servant of St. Andrew'.

Origin of Clan: The Andersons or MacAndrews were first mentioned at the beginning of the 15th century as being part of the Clan Chattan. Clan Anderson has no chief, and is armigerous, meaning that the clan is entitled to bear heraldic arms collectively. Throughout history, the Clan Anderson has been known for its scholarly roots: Alexander Anderson published works on geometry and algebra in Paris between 1612 and 1619 and other family members were skilled in mechanics and mathematics.

Lands: Badenoch, which today forms part of Badenoch & Strathspey in the Highlands.

Arbuthnott ancient

ARBUTHNOTT

Motto: *Laus deo* (Praise be to God).

Heraldic Badge: A peacock's head cut at the neck.

Origin of Name: The name Arbuthnott derived from a region of ancient lands of similar name in Kincardineshire. Early documentation refers to the name as 'Aberbothenoth' which could be translated as 'mouth of the stream below the noble house'.

Origin of Clan: The lands of Arbuthnott are said to have been acquired by Hugh, of the noble family of Swinton, through his marriage to the daughter of Osbert Olifard (Oliphant), known as the 'Crusader'; these events took place during the reign of William of the Lion. In 1282 another Hugh, 'Le Blond', presumably because he had blond hair, became Laird of Arbuthnott. His name appears in a charter of that year as having bestowed land to the monastry of Arbroath to secure his soul a place in heaven.

Lands: Kincardineshire.

Associated Castle: Arbuthnott House, Kincardineshire.

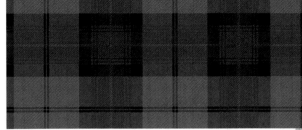

ARMSTRONG

Motto: *Invictus maneo* (I remain unvanquished).

Heraldic Badge: A strong arm.

Origin of Name: A characteristic legend explains how the Armstrong name originated. The name derived from a certain Fairbairn, who, when the King's horse was killed in battle, swung his royal master up onto his own horse. In return the king granted him lands and gave him the name 'Strong-Arm'.

Origin of Clan: The Armstrongs may have been English in origin, having been heard of in Cumbria before there is any mention of them north of the border. Their main centre was Liddesdale, extending by the 16th century into Eskdale and Annandale. The clan is known for its ability to muster 3,000 men when required (certainly an exaggeration). This clan has no chief and is armigerous.

Lands: Liddesdale and throughout the Borders.

Associated Castle: Gilnockie Tower, Dumfries & Galloway.

Baird ancient

BAIRD

Motto: *Dominus fecit* (The Lord has done this).

Heraldic Badge: A gryphon's head.

Origin of Name: The name can be traced to a geographical location in that the Bairds were a family holding lands in Lanarkshire in the 13th century. A characteristic legend ascribes the family's prosperity to an ancestral feat that saved the life of the king, in this case William the Lion (reigned 1165–1214), when threatened by a wild boar killed by Baird's timely spear thrust.

Origin of Clan: The clan origins were in the town of Baird in Lanarkshire, although the Bairds were later to be found in Banffshire and Aberdeenshire where they filled the hereditary office of sheriff for many generations.

Lands: Branches in Aberdeenshire, including Auchmeddan, were later bought by the Earl of Aberdeen. There is a curious prophecy from Thomas the Rhymer that when the eagles, that nested in the crags nearby, disappeared, the estate would pass from the Baird family which, interestingly, came true once the land was sold.

14

Barclay dress

BARCLAY

Motto: *Aut agere aut mori* (Either to do or to die).

Heraldic Badge: A right hand holding a dagger extending from a blue cap.

Origin of Name: The Barclays of Scotland claim to have come to Britain during the Norman Conquest, the name probably originating from the English Berkeley.

Origin of Clan: The founder of the clan is held to be Walter de Berchelai of Gartly, who was Chamberlain of Scotland in the 12th century. Another branch, the Barclays of Mathers, was also descended from an English 'Berkeley', Colonel David Barclay being a leader of the Highlanders who fought for Gustavus Adophus in the Thirty Years' War. He and his descendants became Quakers, and one of them, author of *An Apology for the True Christian Divinity* (1676), was an associate of William Penn, founder of Pennsylvania.

Lands: Kincardineshire, Aberdeenshire.

Associated Castle: Towie Barclay Castle, Aberdeenshire.

BLACK WATCH

Black Watch ancient

Motto: *Nemo me impune lacessit* (No one provokes me with impunity).

Origin of Name: The Black Watch was a Scottish infantry regiment of the British army from 1881 (as the Royal Highland Regiment) to 2006, and was, historically, perhaps the most distinguished in the British army. The Black Watch tartan is perhaps the oldest indisputably authentic tartan, though no one is certain how the sett and colours came to be decided. There is some similarity to the Campbell tartan, and several early commanders were Campbells; but the Black Watch tartan can hardly have derived from the Campbell, more likely the reverse. Similarly, certain so-called hunting tartans may have been based on the Black Watch. None of these tartans was worn when hunting before the Forty-Five (the second Jacobite rebellion of 1745), although Grants sometimes claim that their identical hunting tartan predates the Black Watch. In the early 18th century, the standard dress was the belted plaid, though the kilt (not the Black Watch tartan) was worn off-duty. By tradition, the pipers of the Black Watch wore the Royal Stewart tartan. They seem to have worn a red tartan from the beginning but we can be certain that, in Hanoverian times, it would not have been the Royal Stewart.

Boyd modern

BOYD

Motto: *Confido* (I trust).

Heraldic Badge: A right hand with the last two fingers folded down.

Plant: Laurel.

Origin of Name: The name Boyd was quite common in Arran and Ayrshire and is said to be descriptive, having derived from the Scottish Gaelic for Bute. There is still much speculation as to its precise origin even today.

Origin of Clan: The first recorded Boyds were vassals of the De Morevilles, a powerful Anglo-Norman family in the regality of Largs and Irvine, and possibly came with them from England. Sir Robert Boyd was a supporter of Robert Bruce in his campaign against the English in 1314.

Lands: The Boyds have been associated with lands in Arran and Ayrshire and were appointed earls of Kilmarnock under Charles I; they subsequently lost the title.

Associated Castle: Dean Castle, Ayrshire

17

Brodie modern

BRODIE

Motto: Unite.

Heraldic Badge: A right hand holding a bunch of arrows.

Plant: Periwinkle.

Origin of Name: Derived from the clan's association with the parish of Brodie in Morayshire.

Origin of Clan: The family archives were largely destroyed when Brodie Castle at Forres (now maintained by the National Trust for Scotland) was attacked by forces of Montrose during the campaign of 1645. They were a very old family and, although they can no longer be traced with certainty earlier than the 12th century, it is widely agreed that they were of Pictish origin, there being not many families of whom that can be said. The Brodies of Brodie were active in Scottish affairs during the Middle Ages.

Lands: Morayshire.

Associated Castle: Brodie Castle, Moray.

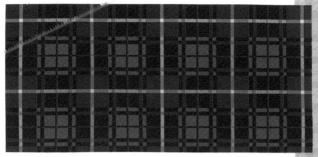

Bruce ancient

BRUCE

Motto: *Fuimus* (We have been).

Heraldic Badge: A standing lion with its tail extended.

Plant: Rosemary.

Origin of Name: The surname Bruce comes from the French de Bruis or de Bruys, derived from the lands now called Brix, situated between Cherbourg and Valognes in Normandy.

Origin of Clan: The de Bruis family arrived with William the Conqueror in 1066. They first settled in the lands of Skelton in Yorkshire, but the Lordship of Annandale was gifted to Robert de Bruis in 1124 through a friendship with King David I. Later generations successively married a daughter and a niece of William the Lion, thus moving closer to the crown.

Lands: Annandale, Clackmannan and Elgin.

Associated Castles: Lochmaben Castle, Dumfries & Galloway; Clackmannan Tower, Clackmannanshire; Broomhall House, Fife.

Buchanan modern

BUCHANAN

Motto: *Clarior hinc honos* (Henceforth the honour shall grow brighter).

War Cry: '*Clar Innes*' (an island in Loch Lomond).

Heraldic Badge: A ducal Cap of Maintenance held in a right fist and surmounted by a rose.

Plant: Bilberry, oak.

Origin of Name: Although the Gaelic version means 'seat of the canon', suggesting a priestly origin, the name actually derives from the district east of Loch Lomond.

Origin of Clan: The clan can trace its line back to Anselan O'Kyan of the Clan Ó Chatháin, a provincial king of north Ulster who landed in Argyll c. 1016. He is traditionally said to have received the lands of Buchanan from King Malcolm II for his services against the Danes. This clan has no chief and is armigerous.

Lands: Stretching to the east and north of Loch Lomond.

Associated Castles: Buchanan Castle, Stirlingshire; Craigend Castle, East Dunbartonshire.

CAMERON

Cameron modern

Motto: *Aonaibh ri cheile* (Unite).

War Cry: *'Chlanna nan con thigibh a so's gheibh sibh feoil'* ('Sons of the hounds come here and get flesh').

Heraldic Badge: A sheath of five arrows.

Plant: Crowberry, oak.

Origin of Name: There are differences of opinion as to the origin of the name, but one popular theory is that it derived from the Gaelic *cam-shron*, which means ' crooked or hooked nose', possibly a reference to the facial features of Donald Dubh, who was the first recorded chief of the clan.

Origin of Clan: The Camerons originally came from three branches. They are one of the greatest Highland clans, but probably share with the Lowland Camerons a common origin in Fife (circumstantial evidence strongly suggests a connection with the old MacDuff earls of Fife).

Lands: Locheil and northern Argyll.

Associated Castles: Achnacarry Castle, Inverness-shire; Tor Castle, Inverness-shire.

21

Campbell ancient

CAMPBELL

Motto: *Ne obliviscaris* (Do not forget).

War Cry: *'Cruachan'* (a mountain near Loch Awe).

Heraldic Badge: A boar's head.

Plant: Bog myrtle.

Origin of Name: The name Campbell derives from the Gaelic *cam-beul*, meaning crooked mouth, and may have been a place name.

Origin of Clan: The Campbells played a major part in local and national affairs from the Middle Ages. Success breeds enemies, and some of the antipathy to the Campbells, still not completely extinct, derives simply from that. Treachery and atrocities were not confined to them, however, and they were adherents of Bruce and later of the Stewart dynasty until the 17th century. Among the oldest of clans, they can reasonably be traced back through the 12th-century Lord of Argyll, Somerled, to the Irish High Kings.

Lands/Branches: Argyll, Cawdor, Loudoun and Breadalbane.

Associated Castles: Castle Campbell, Clackmannanshire; Inveraray Castle, Argyll.

Carnegie modern

CARNEGIE

Motto: Dred [Dread] God.

Heraldic Badge: A winged thunderbolt.

Origin of Name: The name derives from estates in Angus obtained by purchase in the 14th century. The family which adopted this name, however, was originally known under an earlier adopted place name of Bailinhard, which is also in Angus.

Origin of Clan: The Balinhards can be found in records from 1230. In 1358, John of Balinhard was granted the lands and barony of Carnegie by Walter de Maule and became John I of Carnegie. There are several distinguished branches of the family, notably the earls of Ethie (later Northesk), but the most famous Carnegie came from a humbler background. Andrew Carnegie (1835–1919), the great American industrial magnate and philanthropist, was the son of a Dunfermline weaver.

Lands: Angus.

Associated Castles: Kinnaird Castle, Angus; Elsick House, Kincardineshire.

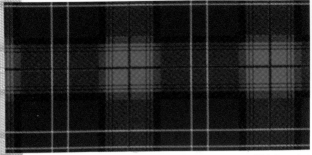

Chisholm ancient

CHISHOLM

Motto: *Feros ferio* (I am fierce with the fierce).

Heraldic Badge: A right hand holding a dagger with a boar's head above.

Plant: Fern.

Origin of Name: The Chisholms take their name from a barony near Hawick in the Borders, where there was a Chisholm of that ilk until the end of the 19th century. In early records the name is written Cheseholm, the name thought to have derived from the Norman French de Chese to which the Saxon *holm* was added upon the marriage of a Norman ancestor to a Saxon heiress.

Origin of Clan: The origins of the clan can be traced to a family which arrived in England after the Norman Conquest of 1066. The Chisholms maintain that only three people are entitled to use the definite article before their names, i.e., 'The Pope, The King and The Chisholm'.

Lands: Roxburghshire and Berwickshire pre-1350, Inverness-shire post-1350

Associated Castle: Erchless Castle, nr. Struy, Highland.

Cochrane ancient

COCHRANE

Motto: *Virtute et labore* (By valour and exertion).

Heraldic Badge: A horse in the walking position with the left foreleg raised.

Origin of Name: The chief of the Cochrane is the Earl of Dundonald, a title created in the early 17th century. The 1st Earl was the son of a man originally named Blair, who married the Cochrane heiress and adopted the family name. The origin of the name itself is derived from two Gaelic words meaning 'battle cry'.

Origin of Clan: Traditionally, the original ancestor of the Clan Cochrane in Scotland was a Scandinavian Viking who settled in what is now Renfrewshire, between the eight and tenth centuries. Nationally, the most famous of recent Cochrane chiefs was the admiral, Lord Cochrane, 10th Earl of Dundonald (1775–1860), who besides notable service for his own country also commanded the naval forces, such as they were, of Chile and Greece during their wars of independence.

Lands: Renfrewshire.

Associated Castles: Auchindoun Castle, Moray; Lochnell Castle, Argyll.

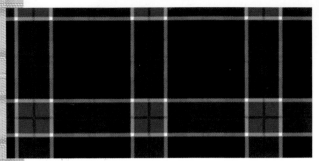

COLQUHOUN

Colquhoun modern

Motto: *Si je puis* (If I can).

War Cry: *'Cnoc Ealachain'* (the clan's rallying place).

Heraldic Badge: A stag's head.

Plant: Dogberry, hazel.

Origin of Name: The name is Irish in origin, the founder of the family being Humphrey of Kilpatrick who obtained the lands in 1241 from the Earl of Lennox in the reign of Alexander II.

Origin of Clan: The Colquhoun lands border Loch Lomond, which was (and is) an attractive region, and also commanded a major route between Highlands and Lowlands. These circumstances may partly account for the particularly bloody history of the Colquhouns, who were a powerful force in the 15th–16th centuries. Of their many feuds, the worst involved the MacGregors.

Lands: Loch Lomond.

Associated Castle: Dunglass Castle, Dunbartonshire.

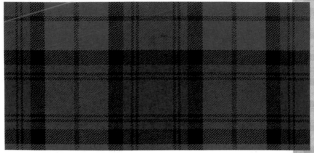

Cranstoun ancient

CRANSTOUN

Motto: *Thou shalt want ere I want.*

Heraldic Badge: A crane (sometimes with head hidden under wing) holding up a stone in its right claw.

Origin of Name: The name has a territorial origin and may have come from the Anglo-Saxon for 'place of the crane', a crane being the bird which appears on both the shield and crest of the Clan Cranstoun. It has also been suggested that the lands were named after the dwelling place of the Cran or Cren, which are both Saxon forenames.

Origin of Clan: The first mention of the name was Elfric de Cranston who is one of the witnesses to a charter by William the Lion in the Abbey of Holyrood in around 1170. The Clan Cranstoun prospered until the late 16th century when it became involved in the volatile political situation of the time. In 1592 Thomas and John Cranstoun were among others accused of treason, with Thomas Cranstoun being executed in 1660.

Lands: Midlothian.

Associated Castle: Corehouse, South Lanarkshire.

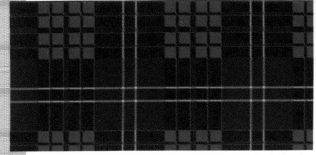

CRAWFORD

Crawford modern

Motto: *Tutum te robore reddam* (I will give you safety by strength).

Heraldic Badge: A stag's head with a cross placed between the antlers.

Origin of Name: The Crawfords or Craufurds are first found in connection with the Barony of Crawford in Lanarkshire, and it is thought that their forebears were among the Norman knights who came to Scotland in the reign of Malcolm III.

Origin of Clan: The Crawfords can be traced to the medieval barony in Lanarkshire. Sir Reginald of Crawford was sheriff of Ayr towards the end of the 12th century. His descendant, Sir John (died 1248), had two daughters, one of whom became the ancestor of the Lindsay earls of Crawford, the other the mother of William Wallace, the leader of the resistance to the English. This clan has no chief and is armigerous.

Lands: Renfewshire, Lanarkshire and Ayrshire

Associated Castles: Auchinames Castle, Renfrewshire; Craufurdland Castle, Ayrshire.

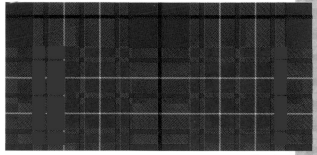

Cumming modern

CUMMING
CUMMIN or COMYN

Motto: Courage.

War Cry: *'An Cuimeanach! An Cuimeanach!'* (A Cumming, a Cumming!).

Heraldic Badge: A lion rampant with a dagger in its paw.

Plant: Cumin.

Origin of Name: Cumming derives from Cummin, possibly a Norman nickname, which was taken from the herb of the same name. The Gaelic name is *Cuimean*. It is also possible that the family took its name from the town of Comines, near Lille, in France.

Origin of Clan: The Cummings or Comyns were the most powerful family in the land at a critical time in Scottish history. William Comyn was an Anglo-Norman magnate who came to Scotland with David I. He was made chancellor, but the founder of the clan was his nephew, Richard, who married a granddaughter of Donald Bán, King of Scots (1093–1097).

Lands: Roxburghshire, Buchan, Badenoch and Altyre.

Associated Castles: Lochindorb Castle, Highland; Inverlochy, Highland.

Cunningham modern

CUNNINGHAM

Motto: Over fork over.

Heraldic Badge: A unicorn's head.

Origin of Name: The name, which first occurs in the 12th century, derives from a district in Ayrshire, although a map dating back to the sixth century shows the original spelling as Canowan. A territorial name, Cunningham derives from the Gaelic *cuinneag* meaning 'milk pail'.

Origin of Clan: The first Cunningham is believed to be a man from Flanders named Wernibald, who assumed the place name as his own when he received a grant of Kilmaurs in Cunningham, Ayrshire, from Hugo de Morville, the Constable of Scotland, in 1140.

Lands: Ayrshire.

Associated Castle: Auchenharvie Castle, Ayrshire; Kerelaw Castle, Ayrshire; Finlaystone Castle, Renfrewshire.

Davidson ancient

DAVIDSON

Motto: *Sapienter si sincere* (Wisely if sincerely).

Heraldic Badge: A stag's head.

Plant: Boxwood, red whortleberry.

Origin of Name: The name derives from the Gaelic word Daibhidh meaning David.

Origin of Clan: The Davidsons are said to have ancient links with the Cummings (Comyns), and after the destruction of the Cummings became a sept of Clan Chattan. They were involved in a long feud with the MacPhersons, among others. In 1370, when the Camerons invaded Clan Chattan territory, Davidson of Invernahaven fell out with Cluny Macpherson over a point of military precedence, with the result that the MacPhersons withdrew and the outnumbered Davidsons were slaughtered. For many years, the chiefship was held by the Davidson of Tulloch who acquired their lands through marriage.

Lands: Ross-shire and Inverness-shire.

Associated Castle: Tulloch Castle, Ross-shire.

Douglas grey

DOUGLAS

Motto: *Jamais arrière* (Never behind).

War Cry: *'A Douglas! A Douglas!'*

Heraldic Badge: A salamander surrounded by fire.

Plant: Rue.

Origin of Name: The name derives from the village of Douglas (Gaelic *Dubh-glas* meaning 'black stream').

Origin of Clan: The Douglases are an ancient clan or noble house from the Scottish Lowlands. Taking their name from Douglas in Lanarkshire, their leaders gained vast territories throughout the Borders, Angus, Lothian, and Moray, and they also had a presence in France and Sweden. This clan has no chief and is armigerous.

Lands: Angus, Lanarkshire, Dumfriesshire, Galloway.

Associated Castles: Douglas Castle, South Lanarkshire; Threave Castle, Dumfries & Galloway; Tantallon Castle, East Lothian.

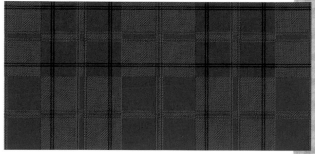

DRUMMOND

Drummond ancient

Motto: *Gang warily* [Go carefully].

Heraldic Badge: A goshawk with wings outstretched within a gold coronet.

Plant: Holly, wild thyme.

Origin of Name: The name derives from the place name, Drymen, near the foot of Loch Lomond. Sir Malcolm de Drymen prospered through support for Bruce, gaining land in Perthshire and Stobhall which was acquired through marriage in 1345.

Origin of Clan: The Drummonds' ancestor was a Hungarian admiral who brought Malcolm Canmore's bride-to-be over from the Continent in 1066 and later married Queen Margaret's Maid-of-Honour. His descendant, Malcolm Beg, Chamberlain of Lennox, was the first documented chief.

Lands: Perthshire.

Associated Castles: Drummond Castle, Perthshire; Balmoral Castle, Aberdeenshire.

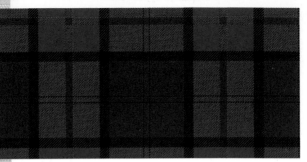

Dunbar ancient

DUNBAR

Motto: *In promptu* (In readiness).

Heraldic Badge: A reined and bridled horse's head.

Origin of Name: The chiefs of Clan Dunbar are of ancient Celtic origin, the town and port of Dunbar having featured prominently in Scottish history on various occasions.

Origin of Clan: Dunbars were to be found at an early date in many parts of Scotland, but the seat of the earls of Dunbar was Dunbar Castle in Lothian, granted to the former Earl of Northumberland (who had been expelled by William the Conqueror) by Malcolm Ceann Mór (Canmore), his first cousin. The Dunbars, who had some claim to the throne themselves, were ill-disposed towards Bruce until after Bannockburn, but the Earl signed the Declaration of Arbroath (1320), the Scottish statement of independence. His wife, 'Black Agnes', held Dunbar Castle for several months against an English siege in 1337.

Lands: East Lothian, Morayshire, Wigtownshire.

Associated Castle: Dunbar Castle, East Lothian.

Duncan ancient

DUNCAN

Motto: *Disce pati (*Learn to endure).

Heraldic Badge: A ship under sail.

Origin of Name: The personal name Duncan can be found in Scotland's oldest records in Gaelic form *Dunchad/Donchadh/Donachie/Donnchadh* and other spelling variants.

Origin of Clan: According to one account, a Clan Donachie/Donnachadh had emerged in the early 14th century from the earls of Atholl, the clan having taken its name from Donnachadh Reamhar, Fat Duncan, who fought at the Battle of Bannockburn, although recent research suggests that this is now unlikely. Duncan's great-grandson was Robert, from whom descends both the Duncans and the Robertsons. The clan has no chief and is armigerous.

Lands: Atholl, Lundie in Fife.

Associated Castle: Camperdown House, Dundee.

DUNDAS

Dundas ancient

Motto: *Essayez* (Try).

Heraldic Badge: A roaring lion's head emerging from a mass of oak leaves.

Origin of Name: *'Dun deas'* in Gaelic means 'south fort'. The Dundas family occupied lands on the southern shores of the Firth of Forth near Edinburgh.

Origin of Clan: The origins of the chiefs of Clan Dundas are thought to rest with Helias, son of Utred, son of Gospatrick, Prince of Northumberland. It is during the reign of William the Lion, however, that the first reliable record of the family is to be found, when Serle de Dundas and Robert de Dundas both appear on the Ragman Rolls swearing fealty to Edward I of England. During the 15th century Sir Archibald Dundas was a favourite of James III of Scotland and was sent by him on several important missions to England. The king intended to give high rank to Dundas but died before he could do so.

Lands: Midlothian.

Associated Castle: Dundas Castle, Edinburgh.

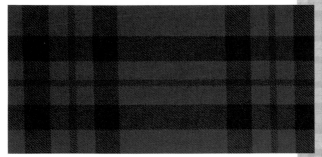

ELLIOT

Elliot ancient

Motto: *Fortiter et recte* (Boldly and rightly).

Heraldic Badge: An armour-clad arm, the hand brandishing a broadsword.

Plant: White hawthorn.

Origin of Name: The name is thought to be of Breton origin and associated with William the Conqueror's army of 1066, which had a large contingent of Elliots and others with similar names, such as Alliot and Elligott.

Origin of Clan: The Elliots were a notorious Borders clan whose territory was in upper Liddesdale, from where they conducted their raids against their neighbouring Scots and English for centuries. At times, the Elliots of Redheugh, the leading family, held that formidable landmark of the Borders, Hermitage Castle, south of Hawick. The origin of the Elliots is obscure in that they suddenly appear as a distinct clan with a chief in the late 15th century. The lack of information is believed to be due to the destruction of their old castle at Stobs in a fire in 1712, in which virtually all the family documents were lost.

Lands: Borders.

Associated Castle: Redheugh Tower, Roxburghshire.

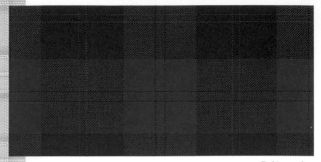

Erskine modern

ERSKINE

Motto: *Je pense plus* (I think more).

Heraldic Badge: A hand holding up a skene rises from an ermine-trimmed cap.

Plant: Red rose.

Origin of Name: The surname Erskine was originally derived from the lands of Erskine, which is an area to the south of the River Clyde in Renfrewshire. The name is believed to derive from the Celtic for 'high, green ground'.

Origin of Clan: Strictly speaking, the Erskines were not chiefs of a genuine clan, their destiny being closely linked with that of the Stewarts. Sir Robert Erskine was Chamberlain of Scotland in the 14th century, and his grandson, the 1st Lord Erskine, claimed the vacant earldom of Mar, an ancient Pictish title, which was not confirmed for several generations.

Lands: Alloa.

Associated Castle: Alloa Tower, Clackmannanshire.

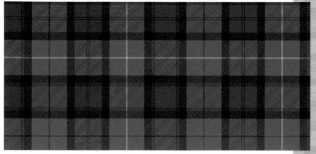

FARQUHARSON

Motto: *Fide et fortitudine* (By fidelity and fortitude).

War Cry: *'Carn na Cuimhne'* (Cairn of Remembrance).

Heraldic Badge: A lion, brandishing a sword in its front right paw, rises from an ermine-trimmed cap.

Plant: Scots fir, foxglove, red whortleberry.

Origin of Name: The Gaelic name *Mac Fhearchair* means 'son of the dear one'.

Origin of Clan: The Farquharsons were a branch of the Shaws and members of the Clan Chattan. They took their name from Farquhar, son of a Shaw chief, and their acknowledged founder was Finlay, who died fighting the English at the Battle of Pinkie (1547). A Celtic harp, the instrument that preceded the pipes in the Highlands, which is now in the National Museum of Antiquities, is said to have been given to Finlay's widow by Mary, Queen of Scots.

Lands: Invercauld, Aberdeenshire.

Associated Castles: Invercauld Castle, Aberdeenshire; Braemar Castle, Aberdeenshire.

Ferguson ancient

FERGUSON

Motto: *Dulcius ex asperis* (Sweeter after difficulties).

Heraldic Badge: A bee resting on a thistle set over an ermine-trimmed cap.

Plant: Pine, poplar.

Origin of Name: The name Ferguson or Fergusson was broadly distributed in Scotland at an early date, and it would be hard to ascribe all the 'sons of Fergus' to a single ancestor. The most notable family, Ferguson of Kilkerran, north-east of Girvan, was regarded as chief by other Fergusons in the south-west. Scottish Gaelic for Ferguson is *MacFhaerghuis*, which can be translated as 'Son of a Stong Man'.

Origin of Clan: The Fergusons of Argyll claim descent from Fergus Mór, King of Dalriada, who came from Ireland across to Argyll. There is evidence that links the Fergusons of Ayrshire and Dumfries with Fergus of Galloway, who was an important figure during the reigns of David I of Scotland and Malcolm IV of Scotland.

Lands: Argyll, Perthshire, Dumfriesshire, Galloway and the estate of Raith.

Associated House: Kilkerran House, Ayrshire.

Forbes ancient

FORBES

Motto: Grace me guide.

War Cry: '*Lonach*' (a mountain in Strathdon).

Heraldic Badge: A stag's head with ten-tined antlers.

Plant: Broom.

Origin of Name: The name Forbes, reputedly in possession of this family since the time of King William the Lion, is most probably a location name assumed from the parish of Forbes in Aberdeenshire, .

Origin of Clan: While there are many legends surrounding the origins of this clan, the first person on record was Duncan Forbes, who in 1271–72 received a grant of lands from Alexander III of Scotland. Traditionally, there is a connection with the Urquharts and possibly the Grants.

Lands: Aberdeenshire.

Associated Castle: Culloden House, Inverness; Castle Forbes, Aberdeenshire; Pitsligo Castle, Aberdeenshire.

Fraser modern

FRASER

Motto: All my hope is in God.

War Cry: '*A Mhór-fhaiche*' *(*the Great Field).

Heraldic Badge: Various parts of the strawberry plant.

Plant: Yew.

Origin of Name: The name is of French origin, and the earliest known Frasers were probably descended from an Angevin named Frezel, a name derived from the French *fraisier*, meaning strawberry plant.

Origin of Clan: The early genealogy suggests a connection with Keith, Lothian, where Simon Fraser held land. About five generations later, another Simon Fraser was captured fighting for the Bruce and was executed in 1306 by Edward I of England. Simon's cousin was Alexander Fraser of Cowie who was Bruce's chamberlain. His younger brother was another Sir Simon, from whom the chiefs of Clan Fraser of Lovat are descended.

Lands: East Lothian, Aberdeenshire.

Associated Castles: Cairnbulg Castle, Pitsligo Castle, Aberdeenshire; Oliver Castle, Scottish Borders.

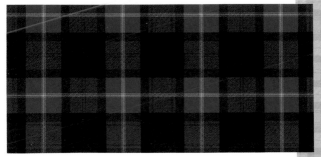

GORDON

Motto: *Bydand* [Steadfast].

War Cry: '*A Gordon!, A Gordon!*'.

Heraldic Badge: A frontal image of a stag's head with ten-tined antlers set over a coronet.

Plant: Ivy.

Origin of Name: From the parish of Gordon in Berwickshire.

Origin of Clan: The first mention is of Richard de Gordon, previously Swinton, said to have been the grandson of a famous knight who slew a monstrous creature during the time of King Malcolm III of Scotland, and who probably died in around 1200. Much of his lands were passed to his son, Thomas Gordon. Other notable Gordons from this time include Bertram de Gordon who wounded King Richard of England with an arrow at Châlons.

Lands: Strathbogie, Deeside, Aberdeen.

Associated Castles: Aboyne Castle, Aberdeenshire; Huntley Castle, Aberdeenshire.

GRAHAM

Graham of Montrose ancient

Motto: *Ne oublie* (Do not forget).

Heraldic Badge: A falcon attacking a stork.

Plant: Laurel.

Origin of Name: The name comes from an English manor whose proprietor, William de Graham ('Grey home'), acquired Abercorn and Dalkeith under David I in the 12th century.

Origin of Clan: There is a tradition that the first Graham was one Greme, who breached the Antonine Wall, driving the Roman legions out of Scotland, although the more likely origin is that the chiefs of Clan Graham were of Anglo-Norman origin. The Manor of Gregham is recorded in William the Conqueror's Domesday Book.

Lands: North of Glasgow, Loch Katrine in the Trossachs, Perthshire, Montrose.

Associated Castles: Mugdock Castle, Stirlingshire; Buchanan Castle, Stirlingshire.

Grant modern

GRANT

Motto: Stand Fast.

War Cry: *'Stand Fast, Craig Elachie!'*

Heraldic Badge: An image of a burning hill. (The burning hill represents 'Craig Elachie', the rallying point of the Grants).

Plant: Pine.

Origin of Name: The origin of the name is the French, *grand*, but the Grants claim an ancient lineage as members of Siol Alpin, the stock of (Kenneth) MacAlpin, and kin to the MacGregors.

Origin of Clan: It is almost certain that the ancestors of the chiefs of Clan Grant first came with the Normans to England where the name is found soon after the conquest of that country. The first Grants to appear in Scotland are recorded in the 13th century when they acquired the lands of Stratherrick.

Lands: Strathspey, Glen Urquhart, Glen Moriston and Loch Ness.

Associated Castle: Castle Grant, Highland.

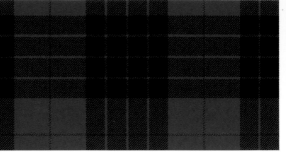

GUNN

Motto: *Aut pax aut bellum* (Either peace or war).

Heraldic Badge: A right hand wielding a sword.

Plant: Juniper.

Origin of Name: The name is of Norse origin, and the possible progenitor of the Gunns was a Norse earl of Orkney, who inherited land in Caithess and Sunderland in the late 12th century.

Origin of Clan: Clan Gunn was never large, although it was involved in long and bloody feuds with powerful neighbours, particularly the Keith, and later the Mackays and the Sinclairs. They were largely dispersed during the Clearances in the early 19th century. This clan has no chief and is armigerous.

Lands: Caithness, Sutherland.

Associated Castle: Castle Gunn/Castle Clyth, Caithness.

Hamilton modern

HAMILTON

Motto: Through.

Heraldic Badge: Set over a ducal coronet, an oak tree bearing acorns is being penetrated transversely in the main stem by a frame saw.

Plant: Oak tree.

Origin of Name: The name derives from the place name, Hameldone, a town in the north of England.

Origin of Clan: Hamilton is a famous name in British history, though not, except in a restricted sense, of a Highland clan. A minor Northumbrian lord, Fitz Gilbert of Hameldone, who also held land in the Lowlands, profited from his support of Bruce in the wars of independence and acquired the barony of Cadzow, later Hamilton.

Lands: Renfrewshire, Arran, South Lanarkshire.

Associated Castles: Hamilton Palace, South Lanarkshire; Lennoxlove House, East Lothian.

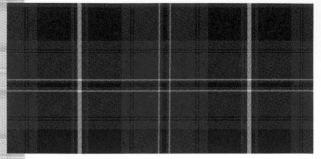

HAY

Hay modern

Motto: *Serva jugum* (Keep the yoke).

War Cry: '*A Hay! A Hay!*'

Heraldic Badge: A flying falcon set over a coronet.

Plant: Mistletoe.

Origin of Name: The name originated in Normandy, from where a powerful family, called the de la Haye, came with William the Conqueror to England in 1066. The name means hedge or stockade, and was not translated into the English language.

Origin of Clan: By 1160 the Hays were well established in Scotland. William de la Haye was cupbearer to Malcolm IV. Their son David integrated the line further into the ruling classes by marrying Ethna, daughter of the Earl of Strathearn, one of Scotland's most ancient earldoms. The chief of Clan Hay holds the hereditary title of Lord High Constable, and enjoys precedence over all other hereditary peers in Scotland.

Lands: Aberdeenshire, Tweeddale.

Associated Castle: New Slains Castle, Aberdeenshire.

Henderson ancient

HENDERSON
OR MACKENDRICK

Motto: *Sola virtus nobilitat (*Virtue alone ennobles).

War Cry: *'The Hendersons are here!'*

Heraldic Badge: An arm, the hand holding a six-pointed star surmounted by a crescent.

Plant: Cotton grass.

Origin of Name: The clan's Gaelic name is *Mac Eanrui*g (MacKendrick) while Henderson is a derivation of 'Henry's Son'.

Origin of Clan: The Hendersons are said to have lived in Glencoe before the MacIain MacDonalds, whom they served as bodyguards and pipers. There were other groups of Hendersons or Mackendricks (the names are the same in Gaelic), not all connected, as far apart as Caithness (where they formed a sept of Clan Gunn) and the Borders, where they were apparently connected with the Elliots.

Lands: Caithness, Glencoe, Borders.

Associated Castle: Fordell Castle, Fife.

Home ancient

HOME

Motto: A Home, a Home, a Home!

Heraldic Badge: A lion's head resting on a ermine-trimmed cap.

Plant: Broom.

Origin of Name: Home is an older variant spelling of Hume, which is a Scottish surname that derives from Hume Castle, Berwickshire, and its adjacent estates. There was an association with the Douglases in the 14th–15th centuries. Some Homes, including the philosopher David Hume, changed the spelling of their name to agree with the pronunciation.

Origin of Clan: The clan descended from Patrick, son of the Earl of Dunbar, who lived in the early 13th century. The Homes frequently held the office of Warden of the March, and they probably deserve some of the credit for the fact that the anarchy of the Borders was less pronounced in the east of their territory than the west.

Lands: The Borders.

Associated Castles: Fast Castle, Berwickshire; Hume Castle, Berwickshire.

INNES

Innes ancient

Motto: Be traist [Be faithful].

Heraldic Badge: A boar's head.

Plant: Great bulrush.

Origin of Name: The name derives from the Gaelic name for an island called Innis which is situated within the Clan Innes territory.

Origin of Clan: The Innes clan can be traced back to a Fleming named Berowald, who gained the barony of Innes, on the Moray Firth, by charter of Malcolm IV in 1160. Thanks largely to well-judged marriages, the chiefs of Innes amassed considerable territory, and branches were established all over the north; but the progress of the line was less smooth than tradition maintained. The 18th Chief was killed in a quarrel with his kinsmen over the chiefship in the 16th century, and a 17th-century successor met his death after having been betrayed by his own son.

Lands: Morayshire.

Associated House: Innes House, Morayshire.

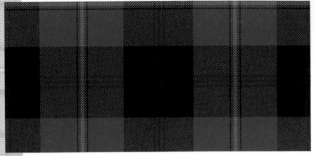

JOHNSTONE

Johnstone ancient

Motto: *Nunquam non paratus* (Never unprepared).

Heraldic Badge: A winged spur rowel.

Plant: Red hawthorn.

Origin of Name: Johnstone is a common name of territorial origin ('John's tun'), and it is clear that not all Johnstones were related. The notable Borders clan used to meet in Devil's Beef Tub, near Moffat, at the head of Annandale, but it was also to be found in neighbouring dales and became divided into numerous branches.

Origin of Clan: The Clan Johnstone was once one of the most powerful of the Borders Reiver Scottish clans. It originally settled in Annandale and for over 600 years held extensive possessions in the west of the Scottish Marches, where it kept watch against the English.

Lands: Aberdeenshire, Borders.

Associated Castles: Lockwood Tower, Dumfries & Galloway; Raehills, Dumfries & Galloway.

Keith ancient

KEITH

Motto: *Veritas vincit* (Truth conquers).

War Cry: *'A Keith, veritas vincit'*.

Heraldic Badge: A roebuck's head rises from a coronet.

Plant: White rose.

Origin of Name: The name is of territorial origin and is from the place name for the lands of Keith in East Lothian.

Origin of Clan: The Keiths, an ancient Celtic family, held the hereditary title of Marischal, later Earls Marischal of Scotland for about 600 years. They held land in Buchan, and in the 14th century, marriage to the heiress of Ackergill took them to Caithness, where they were involved in a long and relentless feud with Clan Gunn. They became more powerful in the time of Bruce by acquiring land all over the country.

Lands: Caithness, East Lothian.

Associated Castles: Keith Marischal, East Lothian; Dunnottar Castle, Aberdeenshire; Fetteresso Castle, Kincardineshire.

53

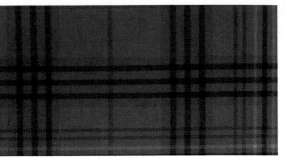

Kennedy ancient

KENNEDY

Motto: *Avise la fin* (Consider the end).

Heraldic Badge: A swimming dolphin.

Plant: Oak.

Origin of Name: It is possible that the name comes from the Gaelic word *ceannaideach*, meaning 'ugly head', although there are other interpretations.

Origin of Clan: The home of the Kennedys is Carrick in Strathclyde, and they appear to be connected with the ancient Celtic Lords of Galloway, who augmented their possessions by marrying useful heiresses, including the daughter of Robert II, which brought them to national prominence. There were also Kennedys in the Highlands, said to be descendants of a fugitive from justice who fled to Lochaber.

Lands: Ayrshire, Lochaber, Skye.

Associated Castles: Cassillis House, Ayrshire; Dunure Castle, Ayrshire; Culzean Castle, Ayrshire.

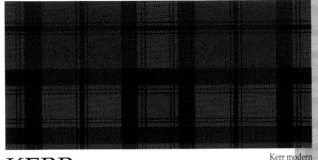

Kerr modern

KERR

Motto: *Sero sed serio* (Late but in earnest).

War Cry: *'Late but in earnest'*.

Heraldic Badge: The sun in all its splendour.

Plant: Bog myrtle.

Origin of Name: Versions of the name were common in the medieval Borders, and probably came from more than one source.

Origin of Clan: The two chief houses of the Kerrs are believed to have derived from two 14th-century brothers, Ralph, ancestor of the Kerrs (or Kers) of Ferniehirst, and John, ancestor of the Kerrs of Cessford. The two strongholds were only 6 miles apart in Teviotdale, and though they sometimes joined forces against the English, they fought one another with equal ferocity. One or other often held the office of Warden of the Middle March.

Lands: Roxburghshire.

Associated Castle: Ferniehirst Castle, Berwickshire.

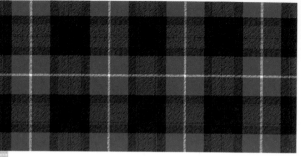

LAMONT

Lamont modern

Motto: *Ne parcas nec spernas* (Neither spare nor dispose).

Heraldic Badge: A right hand cropped at the wrist.

Plant: Crab apple tree.

Origin of Name: The Lamonts came from Cowal and were probably connected with the original King Comgal (died 537). The clan took its name from Ladman, a grandson of Ferchar, who was a chief in Cowal in the late 12th century and spread into Argyll.

Origin of Clan: The clan is said to be descended from Ánrothán Ua Néill, an Irish prince of the O'Neill dynasty. Clan Lamont's historical record is a prominent one: for centuries it ruled almost all the rugged lands of the Cowal peninsula in Argyll, although the clan was severely crippled in 1646, when Campbell clansmen brutally murdered around 200 Clan Lamont members, destroying the seat of Toward on Bute.

Lands: Argyll, Cowal.

Associated Castle: Toward Castle, Argyll.

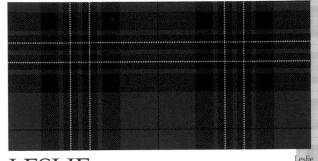

Leslie

LESLIE

Motto: Grip fast.

War Cry: *'Ballinbreich'*.

Heraldic Badge: A rampant gryphon.

Plant: Rue.

Origin of Name: The name comes from a place in Garioch, north-west of Aberdeen. It is uncertain that all Leslies were related to the early lairds of Leslie.

Origin of Clan: The family of Leslie is first found in the late 12th century in the parish of Leslyn or Leslie and was ennobled in 1457 when George Leslie of Rothes was made Earl of Rothes and Lord Leslie. Later earls played a prominent part in national affairs, especially in the 16–17th centuries.

Lands: Aberdeenshire.

Associated Castles: Ballinbreich Castle, Fife; Leslie Castle, Aberdeenshire.

Lindsay modern

LINDSAY

Motto: *Endure fort* (Endure boldly).

Heraldic Badge: A swan rises from a ducal coronet.

Plant: Rue, lime tree.

Origin of Name: The Lindsays were Lowlanders whose name derived from a district in England. Sir Walter de Lindsay was associated with the future David II, when he was in England, and his successor acquired the lands of Crawford in Clydesdale.

Origin of Clan: The family held lands on both sides of the Border until the Wars of Scottish Independence. Their support of Bruce lost them their English estates, but they acquired more lands in Angus, and became earls of Crawford in 1398. The 1st Earl was a famous champion who unhorsed the English champion so easily at a tournament that the English suspected trickery.

Lands: Borders, Angus.

Associated Castles: Crawford Castle, South Lanarkshire; Edzell Castle, Angus.

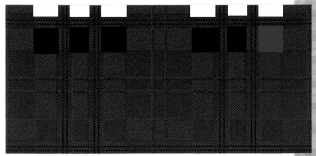

Livingstone modern

LIVINGSTONE

Motto: *Si je puis* (If I can).

Heraldic Badge: A bearded demi-savage, wreathed with laurel and holding a club and serpent.

Origin of Name: The name derives from the district in West Lothian. (Lowlanders often spelled it, like the town, without the final 'e').

Origin of Clan: Sir William Livingstone acquired the barony of Callander and his descendants included the 1st Lord Livingstone in the 15th century. The 5th Lord Livingstone and his son were associated with Mary, Queen of Scots, and James VI made the 7th Lord Earl of Linlithgow in 1600. The 4th Earl fought in the Jacobite rising of 1715 and lost the title, as did the earls of Callander, a separate line descended from the 1st Earl of Linlithgow. The origin of the Highland Livingstones is uncertain, and theories linking them with their Lowland namesakes cannot be trusted.

Lands: West Lothian, Trossachs, Lorne.

Associated House: Bachuil, Isle of Lismore, off Argyll.

LOGAN
OR MACLENNAN

Motto: *Hoc majorum virtus* (This is the valour of my ancestors).

War Cry: *'Druim-nan-Deur'*, the Ridge of Tears.

Heraldic Badge: A passion-nail piercing a human heart.

Plant: Furze (gorse).

Origin of Name: The name Logan is a territorial one derived from the lands of Logan in Ayrshire.

Origin of Clan: There are two branches of the family: the Highland clan usually takes the name MacLennan and the Lowland clan, which takes the name Logan, descends from Sir Robert Logan of Restalrig, who married a daughter of Robert II and in 1400 became Admiral of Scotland. The clan does not have a chief and is armigerous.

Lands: Berwickshire, Lothian, Easter Ross.

Associated Castle: Fast Castle, Berwickshire (was taken by the Homes).

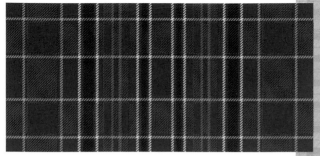

MACALISTER

MacAlister modern

Motto: *Fortiter* (Boldly).

Heraldic Badge: A right hand, the arm clad in armour, holds aloft a dagger.

Plant: Heather.

Origin of Name: The MacAlisters of Loup, a name meaning 'bend', which apparently referred to a feature of its territory, was a branch of Clan Donald, being descended from a great-grandson of Somerled, ancestor of Clan MacDonald.

Origin of Clan: The MacAlisters lived in Kintyre, where Charles MacAlister was appointed steward by James III in 1485, and spread into Arran and Bute. Notable cadet branches were the MacAlister of Tarbert, hereditary constables of the castle of Tarbert on the border between Kintyre and Knapdale, and the MacAlister of Menstrie, who became earls of Stirling, recognized by some MacAlisters as chief of the clan. The MacAlisters of Loup were supporters of the Stewart kings.

Lands: Kintyre, Arran & Bute.

Associated House: Kennox House, Ayrshire.

MacAlpine ancient

MACALPINE

Motto: '*Cuimhnich bas Ailpein*' (Remember the death of Alpin).

War Cry: '*Cuimhnich bas Ailpein*'

Heraldic Badge: A fir tree, surmounted by a Highland broadsword, or claymore, on the point of which a royal crown of Scotland is balanced.

Plant: Pine.

Origin of Name: Son of Alpin. The name is derived from the Gaelic Mac Ailpin. Spelling variations of this name include MacAlpine, MacAlpin, MacAilpein (Gaelic) and others.

Origin of Clan: Siol Ailpein (the race of Ailpein) is very ancient indeed, and covers all those who claim descent from King Alpin, the King of Dalriada, who was slain by Brude of Pictland in AD 834. His son Kenneth can therefore be considered the first King of Scotland.

Lands: Dunstaffnage, Argyll & Bute.

MACARTHUR

MacArthur modern

Motto: *Fide et opera* (By faith and work).

War Cry: *'Eisd! O Eisd!'* (Listen! O Listen!).

Heraldic Badge: Two laurel branches placed curving towards the middle.

Plant: Wild myrtle, fir club moss.

Origin of Name: The MacArthurs came from Argyll and were probably of the same stock as the Campbells. They claimed to be descended from the legendary King Arthur of the Round Table, and if that is hard to swallow, it is no more so than the claim of a Campbell genealogist to have traced his ancestors back to the Egyptian pharaohs.

Origin of Clan: Clan MacArthur, also Clan Arthur, has been described as one of the oldest in Argyll. Clan MacArthur and Clan Campbell share the same origin.

Lands: Argyll, Cowal and Skye.

Associated Castle: Dunstaffnage Castle, Oban.

63

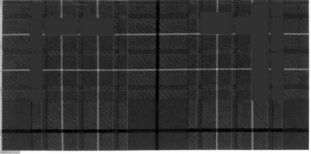

MacAulay modern

MACAULAY

Motto: *Dulce periculum* (Danger is sweet).

Heraldic Badge: A boot with spur attached.

Plant: Cranberry, scots fir.

Origin of Name: The name derives from the Gaelic *Amlaidh Mac Amlaidh* (Aulay MacAulay). Clan MacAulay, also spelt Macaulay or Macauley, is historically centred on the lands of Ardincaple. This clan has no chief and is armigerous.

Origin of Clan: Clan MacAulay has been considered a 'Highland clan' by writers and has been linked by varioius historians to the original earls of Lennox and, in later times, Clan Gregor. There is no connection with the MacAulays of Lewis, whose name meant 'son of Olaf', presumably Olaf the Black, the Norse King of Man and the Western Isles.

Lands: Argyll and Bute.

Associated Castle: Ardincaple Castle, Argyll & Bute.

MacBean ancient

MACBEAN
OR MACBAIN

Motto: *Touch not a catt bot a targe* (Touch not the cat [without] a shield).

War Cry: *'Kinchyle'.*

Heraldic Badge: A wildcat with a Highland shield on its left foreleg.

Plant: Boxwood, red whortleberry.

Origin of Name: Although clan chiefs can be traced to the 15th century, the origin of the name is unknown, although there are plenty of theories. There is evidence, however, that it could be Gaelic in origin.

Origin of Clan: There were MacBeans in the Inverness area under the protection of Mackintosh towards the end of the Middle Ages who are thought to have moved into Clan Chattan territory as a result of intermarriage. Great warriors, the MacBeans feature in many notable battles.

Lands: Inverness-shire.

Associated Castles: Kinchyle Castle, Inverness-shire; Tulloch Castle, Ross-shire, later taken by the Davidsons.

MacBeth ancient

MACBETH

Motto: *Conjuncta virtuti fortuna* (Fortune joined with bravery).

Heraldic Badge: A dragon holding a sword.

Origin of Name: The name MacBeth is likely to have come from the Gaelic *Mac Beatha*, meaning 'Son of Life', but could also possibly have come from the name Béthune, which is a small town in northern France. Both MacBeth and Béthune may have been anglicized to Beaton.

Origin of Clan: The earliest records of the Macbeths place them on the Isle of Islay in the 9th century, where the founder, Macbeth or *Mac Bethad mac Findláich* (1005-57) resided, who was the High Steward of Moray and the last Celtic king of Scotland. In the 16th and 17th centuries, two families, the MacBeths and Bethunes or Beatons, were hereditary physicians to the chiefs of the MacDonald of the Isles. This clan has no chief, and is armigerous.

Lands: Isle of Islay, Isle of Mull, Isle of Skye, Sutherland, Inverness-shire and Easter Ross.

MacCallum ancient

MACCALLUM
OR MALCOM

Motto: *In ardua tendit* (He has attempted difficult things).

Heraldic Badge: A fortified tower.

Plant: Mountain ash.

Origin of Name: MacCallum and Malcolm, according to some theories, are two distinct names, both appearing to derive from 'Colm', no less a figure than St. Columba, who brought Christianity to Scotland in the sixth century.

Origin of Clan: The MacCallum and the Malcolm are both Highland clans. The Clan MacCallum may originally have been a separate clan until the 18th century, when the chief of the Clan MacCallum adopted the name Malcolm, after inheriting the Malcolm estate, and the two clans were drawn together under the same chief.

Lands: Dumbartonshire, Stirlingshire, Argyll.

Associated Castle: Duntrune Castle, Argyll.

MACDONALD

MacDonald ancient

Motto: *Per mare per terras (*By sea and by land).

War Cry: *'Fraoch Eilean' (*The heathery isle).

Heraldic Badge: Over a coronet, a right hand, clad in an armoured gauntlet, holds aloft a cross.

Plant: Heather.

Origin of Name: The name derives from the Gaelic *Domhnuill* meaning 'World Ruler'.

Origin of Clan: Clan Donald, the greatest of the Highland clans, was originally one, but some branches became substantial, independent clans themselves. The name MacDonnell is simply a variant. The original Donald was the grandson of Somerled, who built his principality in Argyll, including Arran and Bute, and the southerly inner Hebrides.

Lands: The Western Isles.

Associated Castles: Armdale Castle (House), Skye; Knock Castle, Skye; Aros Castle, Isle of Mull; Claig Castle, Isle of Jura; Kildonan Castle, Isle of Arran.

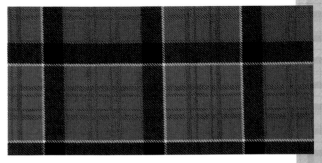

MACDONALD
OF CLANRANALD

MacDonald of Clanranald ancient

Motto: My hope is constant in thee.

War Cry: *'Dh'aindeoin co' theireadh e'* (Gainsay who dare).

Heraldic Badge: A right arm, clad in armour and grasping a sword, issues from a triple-towered castle.

Plant: Heather.

Origin of Name: The name derives from the Gaelic *Domhnuill* meaning 'World Ruler'.

Origin of Clan: MacDonald of Clanranald was Ranald, eldest son of the 1st Lord of the Isles by his first wife. (Ranald did not inherit the lordship, which went to his younger half-brother, whose mother was a daughter of the first Stewart monarch.) For centuries, the stronghold of Clanranald was the fortress of Eilean Tioram in Loch Moidart.

Lands: Northern Isles, north-west Argyll.

Associated Castle: Castle Tioram, Highland.

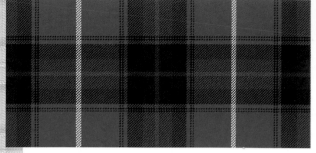

MACDONALD
OF THE ISLES

Motto: *Per mare per terras* (By land and by sea).

Heraldic Badge: On a crest coronet, a right hand, clad in an armoured gauntlet, holds aloft a cross.

Plant: Heather.

Origin of Name: The name derives from the Gaelic *Domhnuill* meaning 'World Ruler'.

Origin of Clan: The first MacDonald of the Isles, John of Islay, descended from Donald, grandson of Somerled, King of the Isles, whose own son, Angus Og, supported Bruce and increased the family and lands significantly. He gained Lewis by royal grant and the southern half of the Outer Hebrides by inheritance through his wife, plus Rhum, and Moidart and Knoydart on the mainland. Having got rid of his productive first wife, he married a daughter of the future King Robert II, which eventually brought him Kintyre and Knapdale.

Lands: The Western Isles.

Associated Castle: Finlaggan Castle (also known as Eilean Mor Castle), Island of Islay.

MACDONALD
OF SLEAT

MacDonald of Sleat ancient

Motto: *Per mare per terras* (By land and by sea).

Heraldic Badge: On a crest coronet, an armoured right hand holds aloft a cross.

Plant: Heather.

Origin of Name: The name derives from the Gaelic *Domhnuill* meaning 'World Ruler'.

Origin of Clan: The first MacDonald of Sleat was Hugh, youngest son of Alexander, 3rd Lord of the Isles. He received Sleat, on Skye, from his father. As in other Highland dynasties, the persistence of the family name, Donald, can be a source of confusion. Donald Gorm, 5th of Sleat, was involved in efforts to retain the inheritance of the lordship in 1539, and was killed besieging the Mackenzie castle of Eilean Donan.

Lands: Skye.

Associated Castles: Dunscaith Castle, Isle of Skye; Duntulm Castle, Isle of Skye; Armadale Castle, Isle of Skye.

MacDonell of Glengarry ancient

MACDONELL
OF GLENGARRY

Motto: *'Creag an Fhitich' (*The raven's rock).

War Cry: *'Creag an Fhitich'.*

Heraldic Badge: A raven perched on a rock.

Plant: Heather.

Origin of Name: The name derives from the Gaelic *Domhnuill* meaning 'World Ruler'.

Origin of Clan: The ruined but still oppressive castle of Invergarry, overlooking Loch Oich, was the stronghold of MacDonell of Glengarry, which was a cadet branch of MacDonald of Clanranald, stemming from Donald, son of Ranald who, despite the cantankerous nature of many Glengarry chiefs, generally shared Clanranald's loyalties. The 6th Glengarry married a daughter of MacDonald of Lochalsh, which gave him a doubtful claim to the chiefship of Clan Donald and involved the clan in a long feud with the expanding Mackenzies.

Lands: Glengarry.

Associated Castles: Strome Castle, Highland; Invergarry Castle, Highland.

MacDonell of Keppoch ancient

MACDONELL
OF KEPPOCH

Motto: *Per mare per terras* (By sea and by land).

War Cry: *'Dia's Naomh Aindrea'* (God and St. Andrew).

Heraldic Badge: A cowned golden eagle.

Plant: White heather.

Origin of Name: The name derives from the Gaelic *Domhnuill* meaning 'World Ruler'.

Origin of Clan: The MacDonells of Keppoch descended from Alastair, third son of John, 1st Lord of the Isles, whose lands were in Lochaber. They took part in the various campaigns and rebellions of the Lords of the Isles, losing some land to the Mackenzies which added to the feud. They remained closely connected with Clanranald and Glengarry, in spite of an incident in 1663 when Glengarry failed to avenge the murder of the 12th MacDonell of Keppoch near Invergarry (vengence was later exacted by MacDonald of Sleat).

Lands: Keppoch, Lochaber.

Associated Castle: Keppoch Castle, Highland.

MACDOUGALL

MacDougal ancient

Motto: *Buaidh no bas* (Victory or death).

War Cry: *'Buaidh no bas'*.

Heraldic Badge: A right arm, clad in armour and resting on an ermine-trimmed cap, holds aloft a cross.

Plant: Bell heather, cypress.

Origin of Name: The name derives from the Gaelic *Dughall* meaning 'black stranger or foreigner'.

Origin of Clan: The MacDougall, once a formidable power in the west, still hold part of their ancient patrimony in Lorn. They are senior to Clan Donald, being descended from Dugall, the eldest son of Somerled. He was the senior sub-king under the Norse King of the Isles and styled himself 'of Argyll'. Necessarily, the future MacDougalls were a sea power, and their original strongholds were Dunstaffnage, which later passed to the Campbells, and Dunollie, above Oban Bay, which they still hold.

Lands: Lorn.

Associated Castle: Dunollie Castle, Argyll.

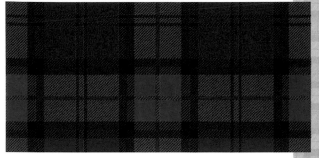

MACDUFF

Motto: *Deus juvat* (God assists).

Heraldic Badge: A seated lion holding aloft a sword.

Plant: Red whortleberry, boxwood.

Origin of Name: The name derives from the Gaelic *Mac-Dubh* meaning 'Son of the Dark One'.

Origin of Clan: The origins of the ancient and exalted Clan MacDuff can be traced back to the earls of Fife in the early 12th century and, by inference, a great deal further. The first documented Earl of Fife was the eldest son of Malcolm Ceann Mór (the MacDuff of Shakespeare's *Macbeth* cannot be historically established although he is certainly feasible). He was also hereditary abbot of Dunkeld and his wife was a granddaughter of Queen Gruoch (Lady Macbeth) and sister of the ruler of Moray. His descendants enjoyed unique privileges, among them the right to enthrone the King of Scots at Scone. This clan has no chief and is armigerous.

Lands: Fife, Lothian, Strathbran, Strathbogie.

Associated Castle: MacDuff's Castle, Fife.

MACEWEN

MacEwen modern

Motto: *Reviresco* (I grow strong again).

Heraldic Badge: The stump of an oak tree sprouting new growth.

Plant: Oak tree.

Origin of Name: The name derives from the personal name of Ewen. The Gaelic form of the name is *MacEòghainn*.

Origin of Clan: The MacEwens seem once to have been a numerous clan, connected with the MacNeils and MacLachlans. In the 18th-century parish records of Kilfinnan in Argyll, there is a mention of a ruined building on Loch Fyne, which was named MacEwen's Castle for a chief who held land in the district of Otter. There appears to have been no other memory of the MacEwens in their own homeland even at that time. This clan has no chief and is armigerous.

Lands: Argyll, Galloway, Lennox, Cowal.

Associated Castle: MacEwen's Castle, Argyll.

MacFarlane ancient

MACFARLANE

Motto: This I'll defend.

War Cry: 'Loch Slòigh' (Loch Sloy).

Heraldic Badge: A naked bearded figure holds aloft a broadsword in the right hand while pointing to a crown with the other.

Plant: Cranberry, cloudberry.

Origin of Name: The name is derived from the 4th Chief, Párlane (Bartholomew), descendant of Gilchrist, who received the lands from his brother, Earl Malduin.

Origin of Clan: The MacFarlanes were descended from the old Celtic earls of Lennox and through them, probably, from the kings of Munster. Their homeland was Arrochar, at the head of Loch Long. This clan has no chief and is armigerous.

Lands: Loch Lomond, Tarbert, Arrochar.

Associated Castles: Thought to have inhabited a castle in Arrochar, Argyll & Bute.

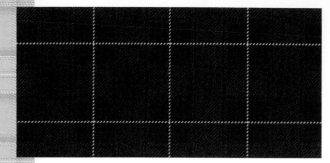

MACFIE

Motto: *Pro rege* (For the king).

Heraldic Badge: A rampant half-lion.

Plant: Oak, crowberry, Scots pine.

Origin of Name: The name derives from the Gaelic *MacDhuibhsith* meaning 'Son of the Dark (One) of Peace'.

Origin of Clan: Little is known of the early history of the clan, but it is certain that it served under the Lord of the Isles – descendants of Somerled, who ruled the Hebrides from the 14th to the late 16th centuries. The ancestral homeland of the Macfies is the islands of Colonsay and Oronsay in the Western Isles of Scotland. This clan has no chief and is armigerous.

Lands: Colonsay, Oronsay.

Associated Castle: Dùn Eibhinn, Island of Colonsay.

MACGILLIVRAY

MacGillivray hunting

Motto: Touch not this cat.

War Cry: *'Dunmaglas'* (The name of the chief's castle).

Heraldic Badge: A wildcat.

Plant: Boxwood, red whortleberry.

Origin of Name: The name derives from the Gaelic *Mac Gillie Bhrath* meaning 'Son of the Servant of Judgement'.

Origin of Clan: The clan is said to have originated in Mull, and some became followers of MacLean of Duart. Another group sought protection from the Mackintosh chief in the mid-13th century, an early example of a process that resulted in the development of the Clan Chattan confederation. The presumed progenitor was Gillebride, or Gillivray, and by the 15th century his descendants held land in Dunmaglas in Strathnairn. This clan has no chief and is armigerous.

Lands: Mull, Lochaber, Morven, Strathnairn, Inverness-shire.

Associated Castle: Dunmaglas Castle, Inverness-shire.

MacGregor ancient

MACGREGOR

Motto: *'S rioghal mo dhream* (Royal is my race).

War Cry: *'Ard-choille'* (The High Wood).

Heraldic Badge: A crowned lion's head.

Plant: Scots pine.

Origin of Name: From the Gaelic *MacGrioghair*, meaning 'Son of Gregory'(son of a shepherd).

Origin of Clan: The MacGregors were the principal members of Síol Alpin, the kin of Kenneth MacAlpin, claiming descent from his brother or son. Their homeland was Glenorchy, where the Campbells had a foothold by the 14th century through marriage. By one means or another, they steadily extended their possessions and the MacGregor chiefs became their tenants. The MacGregors were forced into a lawless existence, defending their land by the sword.

Lands: Eastern Argyll and western Perthshire.

Associated Castles: Kilchurn Castle, Argyll & Bute; Meggernie Castle, Perthshire; Lanrick Castle, Perthshire.

MacInnes hunting ancient

MACINNES

Motto: *Irid Ghift dhe Agus an Righ* (By the Grace of God and the King).

Heraldic Badge: A tartan-clad arm holds aloft a bow.

Plant: Holly.

Origin of Name: The name derives from the Gaelic *MacAonghuis*, 'Son of Angus', meaning 'unique choice'.

Origin of Clan: Clan MacInnes was of ancient origin, and were probably connected with the MacGillivrays; a 17th-century chronicler described them as the same people. Their paths subsequently diverged, the sons of Innes, or Angus, coming under Campbell, rather than Mackintosh protection. The ruins of their castle of Kinlochaline still stand, and a MacInnes was still its constable when it was besieged by Alasdair MacColla (MacDonald) in 1645. This clan has no chief and is armigerous.

Lands: Morven, Ardgour, Skye.

Associated Castle: Kinlochaline Castle, Highland.

MacIntyre hunting

MACINTYRE

Motto: *Per ardua* (Through adversity).

War Cry: *Cruachan!* (A mountain near Loch Awe).

Heraldic Badge: A right hand holding aloft a dagger.

Plant: White heather.

Origin of Name: Colourful legends account for the origin of Clan MacIntyre and for its name. The Gaelic name, *Mac-an t'saor* means 'Son of the Carpenter', which might well have applied to people not related by blood.

Origin of Clan: The MacIntyres were closely connected with the MacDonalds and one legend says that their founder was a MacDonald who cut off his thumb to plug a leak in his boat so that he could wave both arms for help. Wood certainly seems to have been a significant material; the hereditary foresters to the Stewart and later Campbell lords of Lorne were MacIntyres.

Lands: Glenoe.

Associated Castle: Sorn Castle, Ayrshire.

MacKay blue

MACKAY

Motto: *Manu forti* (With a strong hand).

War Cry: *'Bratach Bhan Chlann Aoidh'* (The white banner of the Mackay).

Heraldic Badge: A right hand holding aloft a dagger.

Plant: Bulrush.

Origin of Name: The name derives from the Gaelic *MacAoidh*, meaning 'Son of Fire'.

Origin of Clan: The Mackays claimed descent from the old earls or *mormaers* (a weightier title than the English 'earl') of Moray, although their homeland was in the north, centred on Strathnaver, their movement thither having possibly been the result of the campaigns of King Malcolm IV (1153–1165). It was said that in 1427 their chief, Angus Dubh, who was married to a daughter of Donald, 2nd Lord of the Isles, could command 4,000 men.

Lands: Argyll, Sutherland, Ross.

Associated Castle: Varrich Castle, Highland.

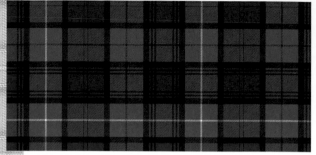

Mackenzie

MACKENZIE

Motto: *Luceo non uro* (I shine, not burn).

War Cry: *Tulach Ard* (A mountain in Kintail).

Heraldic Badge: A mountain being consumed by fire.

Plant: Holly, stagshorn clubmoss.

Origin of Name: The name is derived from the Gaelic *MacCoinnich*, meaning 'Son of the Fair'.

Origin of Clan: Since the 'k' in Mackenzie is an intruder, not present in Gaelic, Mackenzie is one of those names generally spelled without a capital letter following the Mac. The origins of the clan are unknown, though a strong tradition links them with the old royal house of Lorne, and they were a major constituent of Clan Chattan. A royal charter of 1362, which confirms the current chief, Murdoch, in the lands of Kintail, corroborates his descent from Gilleon of the Aird, prince of the house of Lorne.

Lands: Isle of Lewis, Ross and Cromarty.

Associated Castles: Castle Leod, Ross-shire; Eilean Donan Castle, Highland; Redcastle, Ross and Cromarty.

MACKINNON

Motto: *Audentes fortuna juvat* (Fortune assists the daring).

War Cry: *Cuimhnich bas Ailpein* (Remember the death of Alpin).

Heraldic Badge: A boar's head holding a shin-bone in its mouth.

Plant: Scots pine.

Origin of Name: The name derives from the Gaelic *Mac Fhionghuin*, meaning 'Son of Fair Born' or 'Fair Son'.

Origin of Clan: The Mackinnons claim descent both from the family of Kenneth MacAlpin and from St. Columba, and, significantly, the brother of a 14th-century chief was the Abbot of Iona. The last abbot, who died in 1500 (his effigy can still be seen on Iona), was Iain Mackinnon. The Mackinnon homeland was the Isle of Mull, but they acquired, presumably through marriage, a larger area at Strathaird on Skye, plus Scalpay. Their castle of Dunakin (Dunan) guarded the passage between the two islands.

Lands: Skye, Iona, North Mull.

Associated Castle: Caisteal Maol (Dunakin), Isle of Skye.

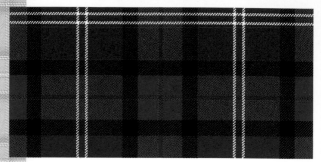

MACKINTOSH

Motto: *Touch not the cat bot with a glove.*

War Cry: *Loch Moigh* (Loch Moy– an island where the former chiefs had their stronghold).

Heraldic Badge: A rearing wildcat.

Plant: Red whortleberry, boxwood.

Origin of Name: The Gaelic name *Mac-an-tòiesch* means 'Son of the Chief', and it was no doubt applied to others besides members of the famous clan which led the confederation known as Clan Chattan.

Origin of Clan: The name first appears as the name of a captain of Clan Chattan in the 15th century, when the chief was based on an island in Loch Moy. He claimed descent from a younger son of MacDuff, ancestor of the old earls of Fife.

Lands: Inverness-shire.

Associated Castles: Moy Castle and Moy Hall, Inverness-shire.

MacLachlan modern

MACLACHLAN

Motto: *Fortis ed fidus* (Brave and faithful).

Heraldic Badge: A triple-towered fortification rises out of a ducal coronet.

Plant: Mountain ash.

Origin of Name: The Gaelic name *MacLachlainn* (Son of Lachlan) possibly comes from Lachlan Mor (a 13th-century chief who lived on the shores of Loch Fyne.

Origin of Clan: According to the Celtic genealogists five generations removed from Aodh O'Neill, King of Ulster in the 11th century, Lachlan, from whom the clan takes its name, had his seat at Castle Lachlan on Loch Fyne, and the MacLachlans were close neighbours of the Campbells. Their survival depended on good relations with that powerful clan, and there were frequent marriages between them.

Lands: Argyll, Perthshire, Lochaber, Stirlingshire.

Associated Castles: Old and New Castle Lachlan, Argyll & Bute.

MACLAINE
OF LOCHBUIE

Maclaine of Lochbuie ancient

Motto: *Vincere vel mori* (To conquer or die).

War Cry: *'Vincere vel mori'*.

Heraldic Badge: A battle-axe flanked by branches of laurel and cyprus.

Plant: Blaeberry (whortleberry), bramble.

Origin of Name: The name derives from *MacGhille-Eoin*, meaning 'Son of the Servant of John'.

Origin of Clan: Clan Maclaine of Lochbuie inhabited the lands on the southern end of the Isle of Mull in the Scottish Highlands. The Maclaines of Lochbuie are descended from Hector, the brother of Lachlan, who founded the Duart branch of the MacLeans, with Hector having acquired the lands of Lochbuie from John 1st Lord of the Isles in the 14th century. The family used the MacLean spelling until about 1600.

Lands: Lochbuie, Isle of Mull.

Associated Castles: Moy Castle, Isle of Mull.

MacLaren modern

MACLAREN

Motto: *Creag an Turic* (The Boar's Rock).

War Cry: *'Creag an Turic'*.

Heraldic Badge: A crowned lion's head flanked by two branches of laurel.

Plant: Laurel.

Origin of Name: The name derives from the Gaelic *MacLabhruinn*, meaning 'Son of Lawrence'.

Origin of Clan: The MacLarens are not well documented, but it is generally accepted that they came from Balquidder and were related to the old earls of Strathearn, the last of whom died in the mid-14th century. They spread a considerable distance, though they never held legal title to their lands, but in the 16th century they were overrun by the MacGregors with terrible slaughter and, probably, the destruction of all clan records.

Lands: Strathearn and Balquidder.

MACLEAN
OF DUART

MacLean hunting modern

Motto: Virtue mine honour.

War Cry: *'Bas no beatha'* (Death or life).

Heraldic Badge: A fortified tower.

Plant: Crowberry.

Origin of Name: The ancestor from whom the MacLeans took their name was Gillean of the Battle-Axe, a 13th-century chieftain descended from the royal house of Lorne.

Origin of Clan: There are two senior branches of MacLean, MacLean of Duart and Maclaine of Lochbuie, founded by two brothers who lived in the late 14th century. MacLean of Duart is generally regarded as the senior house, though there was always some rivalry. In important affairs, the MacLeans normally acted together.

Lands: Isle of Mull, Morven, Lochaber, Tiree, Coll.

Associated Castle: Duart Castle, Isle of Mull.

MacLeod of Harris ancient

MACLEOD

Motto: Hold fast.

Heraldic Badge: A bull's head between two flags.

Plant: Juniper.

Origin of Name: The name derives from the Gaelic *MacLeoed*, meaning 'Son of Leod'.

Origin of Clan: Leod was a son of Olaf the Black (died 1237), the Norse king of Man and the Isles. He acquired Harris, Lewis and part of Skye, including Dunvegan, the home of the chiefs for 700 years. His sons, Tormod and Torquil, were ancestors of the two senior branches of the MacLeods, Síol Thormoid, on Harris, and Síol Thorcail on Lewis. As with the MacLeans, there was rivalry between the two over seniority (in Celtic custom, the eldest son did not have automatic precedence).

Lands: Skye, Lewis, Harris.

Associated Castles: Dunvegan Castle, Isle of Skye; Ardvreck Castle, Sutherland; Dunscaith Castle, Highland.

MacMillan ancient

MACMILLAN

Motto: *Miseris succurrere disco* (I learn to succour the unfortunate).

Heraldic Badge: A sword being brandished with two hands on the hilt.

Plant: Holly.

Origin of Name: The Gaelic name *MacMhaolain* means 'Son of the Shaven-headed One' and the implication is that the founder was a monk (no doubt a high-flying abbot).

Origin of Clan: The MacMillans were to be found in many parts at a comparatively early date and it would be hard to prove that they shared a common ancestor. A substantial clan towards the end of the Middle Ages was MacMillan of Knap (Knapdale), which held a charter from the Lord of the Isles containing a promise, engraved on a rock by Loch Sween, that they should hold the land 'as long as the sea beats on the rock'. The Campbells, however, only acquired Knapdale in the 18th century.

Lands: Argyll, Galloway, Lochaber.

Associated Castle: Finlaystone House, Renfrewshire.

MACNAB

Motto: *Timor omnis abesto* (Let fear be far from all).

Heraldic Badge: A bearded head facing to the front.

Plant: Roebuckberry (stone bramble), heather.

Origin of Name: The name is derived from the Gaelic *Mac An Abu*, which means 'Child of the Abbot'.

Origin of Clan: In the old Celtic Church, high offices were usually hereditary among leading families. Nor was marriage prohibited, so it is not surprising that many clans have an ecclesiastical ancestry. The MacNabs possibly descend from St. Fillan, abbot of Glen Dochart in the seventh century. Though their numbers were not large, the MacNabs were a fierce and independent breed, and their chiefs were men of forceful character, as is evident in Raeburn's great portrait of the 16th McNab (1734–1816).

Lands: Glen Dochart, Loch Tay.

Associated Castles: The ancient seat of the MacNabs was a castle on Eilean Ran, an island on River Lochay; Kinnell House, Perthshire.

MACNAUGHTON
OR MACNACHTAN

MacNaughton ancient

Motto: I hope in God.

War Cry: *'Fraoch Eilean'* (Heathery Isle).

Heraldic Badge: A fortified tower.

Plant: Trailing azalea.

Origin of Name: The name derives from the Gaelic *MacNeachdainn*, meaning 'Son of the Pure One'.

Origin of Clan: The MacNaughtons (variously spelled), were of Pictish stock and were probably resident in Stathtay before the main clan settled in Argyll, between Loch Fyne and Loch Awe, the future heartland of the Cambells. As followers of the MacDougall lords of Lorne, they supported Balliol against Bruce and suffered as a result, but largely regained their position in the 14th century when their headquarters were at Dunderave Castle on Loch Fyne.

Lands: Argyll, Lewis, Strathtay.

Associated Castles: Dunderave Castle, Argyll; Dunderave House, County Antrim, Northern Ireland.

MacNeil ancient

MACNEIL

Motto: *Buaidh no bas* (Victory or death).

War Cry: *'Buaidh no bas'.*

Heraldic Badge: A rock rising from a baron's cap.

Plant: Dryas.

Origin of Name: The name derives from the Gaelic *MacNeill*, meaning 'Son of Neil'.

Origin of Clan: The MacNeils, or MacNeills, inhabited the smaller islands of the Hebrides and were certainly of common ancestry. The MacNeils of Barra claimed descent from the Irish High King, Niall of the Nine Hostages, who lived in the fourth century, but took their name from a later Irish Niall, who lived around 1300. The first documented MacNeil chief had a charter from the Lord of the Isles, and after the collapse of the lordship lived largely by piracy, secure in his stronghold of Kisimul on a rocky island in Castle Bay.

Lands: Barra, Gigha, Knapdale, Colonsay.

Associated Castle: Kisimul Castle, Barra.

MACNICOL
OR NICOLSON

Motto: *Generositate* (By generosity).

War Cry: *'Meminisse sed providere'* (Remember but look ahead).

Heraldic Badge: A hawk's head with tongue extended.

Plant: Juniper.

Origin of Name: The name derives from the Gaelic name *MacNeacall*, meaning 'Son of Nicol'.

Origin of Clan: The MacNicols or Nicolsons are associated with the north-west, Skye in particular, but the name appears frequently in Scotland at a comparatively early date and it is unlikely that all were connected. According to the old Celtic genealogies, the sons of Nicol originated in Assynt and Ullapool on the mainland, probably moving to Skye later and eventually adopting the name Nicolson, rather than MacNicol (closer to the Gaelic).

Lands: Formerly Assynt, later Skye, Argyll.

Associated Castle: Scorrybreac Castle, Isle of Skye.

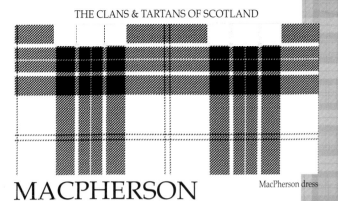

MacPherson dress

MACPHERSON

Motto: Touch not the cat bot [with] a glove.

War Cry: *'Creag Dhubh Chloinn Chatain'* (The Black Rock of Clan Chattain).

Heraldic Badge: A seated wildcat.

Plant: White heather, boxwood.

Origin of Name: The name derives from the Gaelic *Mac a'Phearsoin* 'Son of the Parson'.

Origin of Clan: The McPhersons of Badenoch were rivals of the Mackintoshes, with whom they disputed the captaincy of Clan Chattan. The rivalry was exploited by a succession of powerful neighbours and overlords, the Cummings (Comyns), the Stewarts, and finally the Gordon earls of Huntly. Although MacPherson of Cluny, the senior line, signed the Clan Chattan bond of union in 1609, the clan generally showed little enthusiasm for making common causes with Mackintosh.

Lands: Badenoch.

Associated Castles: Cluny Castle, Aberdeenshire; Newton Castle, Perthshire; Ballindalloch Castle, Banffshire.

MacQuarrie modern

MACQUARRIE

Motto: *An t'Arm Breac Dearg* (The Red-Tartaned Army).

War Cry: '*An t'Arm Breac Dearg*'.

Heraldic Badge: A bent right arm, clad in armour and rising from a coronet, holds aloft a dagger.

Plant: Pine tree.

Origin of Name: The name comes from *guaire*, meaning 'noble' and, according to tradition, refers to a brother of Fingon, ancestor of the MacKinnons.

Origin of Clan: Clan MacQuarrie is an ancient Highland clan whose home was Ulva, off Mull, and they also held Staffa and land on Mull. They were loyal subjects of the Lord of the Isles, later of the royal Stewarts, but were never numerous. They became followers of MacLean of Duart, and were decimated in the battle of Inverkeithing (1651), when the chief and many clansmen were killed. This clan has no chief and is armigerous.

Lands: Ulva, Staffa, Mull.

MacQueen modern

MACQUEEN

Motto: Constant and faithful.

War Cry: Constant and faithful.

Heraldic Badge: A rampant tiger holds an arrow pointed downwards.

Plant: Boxwood, red whortleberry.

Origin of Name: The name derives from the Gaelic, *MacShuibhne* (Son of the Good Going).

Origin of Clan: The MacQueens are of the same descent as their neighbours Clan Donald, having descended from the King of Ireland. They first appear in the 13th century as custodians of Castle Sween in Kintyre. They have long been associated with the MacDonalds of Clanranald and became a strong branch of the Clan Chattan. This clan has no chief and is armigerous.

Lands: Skye, Lewis, Argyll, Lanarkshire.

Associated Castle: Castle Sween, Argyll.

MACRAE

MacRae ancient

Motto: *Fortitudine* (With fortitude).

War Cry: '*Sgur urain*' (A mountain in Kintail).

Heraldic Badge: A right arm brandishing a sword.

Plant: Fir club moss.

Origin of Name: The name is one of many forms of the Gaelic *Mac Rath*, meaning 'Son of Grace', and is unlikely to have anything to do with a particular individual.

Origin of Clan: Clan MacRae is associated above all with Kintail and the castle of Eilean Donan, but not all MacRaes are related to the Highland clan. The MacRaes originally lived near Inverness and were closely linked with the Frasers, but by 1400 they were established in Kintail, Wester Ross, attached to the rising power of the Mackenzies, whom they served as Constables of Eilean Donan castle among other offices.This clan has no chief and is armigerous.

Lands: Beauly, Kintail.

Associated Castle: Eilean Donan, Highland.

MACTAVISH

MacTavish ancient

Motto: *Non oblitus* (Not forgotten).

War Cry: *'Cruach Mór'* (Great Hill).

Heraldic Badge: A boar's head encircled by a strap and buckle (belt).

Origin of Name: The name MacTavish derives from *Mac Tamhais*, which means 'Son of Thomas'. Variant names and septs for Clan MacTavish include Cash, MacCash, MacCavish, MacLehose, MacSteaphain, MacThom, MacThomas, Stephen(son), Steven(son), Tais, Taws, Taweson, Thom, Thomas, Thomason, Thompson, Thomson, Tod(d) and all variant spellings.

Origin of Clan: There are records which trace the clan back to the 12th century where it was based around Argyll. It can be difficult to find accurate information about the origin of this Highland clan, as some accounts have been re-written over the centuries, although the clan can be traced back to the early royal families of Ireland and the Dalriada settlements in the Pictish world.

Lands: Dunardry, Argyll.

Associated Castle: Castle of Dunardry, Argyll.

MATHESON

Matheson modern

Motto: *Fac et spera* (Do and hope).

War Cry: '*Acha 'n da Thearnaidh*' (Field of the Two Declavities).

Heraldic Badge: A right hand rising out of a coronet brandishes a scimitar.

Plant: Broom.

Origin of Name: The name derives from the Gaelic *Mac Mhathain*, meaning 'Son of the Bear'.

Origin of Clan: The name is not uncommon in Scotland, but not all Mathesons are related to the clan whose home was Lochalsh and who claimed descent from the same ancestor as the Mackenzies, Gilleon of the Aird. The Mathesons supported the Lord of the Isle, who also became the earl of Ross in the 15th century.

Lands: Lochalsh, Sutherland.

Associated Castles: Fort Matheson, Highland; Lewis Castle, Isle of Lewis; Ardross Castle, Ross-shire.

Maxwell modern

MAXWELL

Motto: *Reviresco* (1 grow strong again).

Heraldic Badge: A stag lying in front of a holly bush.

Origin of Name: The name derives from the name of a Norse chief called Maccus who gave his name to Maccuswell, a pool in the River Tweed near Kelso in the Scottish Borders.

Origin of Clan: The famous Border clan of Maxwell was probably of English origin. In the 13th century, John of Maccuswell was Chamberlain of Scotland and at that time his family probably already held their famous stronghold of Caerlaverock, in lower Nithsdale. His immediate successors were the ancestors of numerous branches, which were apt to feud among themselves although when kinship was reinforced by feudal obligations, the Maxwells of Caerlaverock were able to command substantial forces. This clan has no chief and is armigerous.

Lands: Borders.

Associated Castles: Threave Castle, Dumfries & Galloway; Maxwell's Castle; Dumfries & Galloway; Caerlaverock Castle, Dumfries & Galloway.

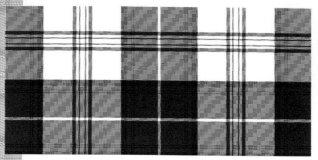

Menzies red & white ancient

MENZIES

Motto: *Vil God I zal (Will God I shall).*

War Cry: *'Geal us Derg a suas' (*Up with the White and Red).

Heraldic Badge: A front-facing bearded head.

Plant: Heather, mountain ash.

Origin of Name: Usually pronounced 'mingess' the name, which has several variants in Scotland, including Meyners, appears to be of Anglo-Norman origin and is equivalent to the English Manners.

Origin of Clan: The name first appeared in Lothian but the clan was established in Atholl in the 13th century and, after the success of Bruce, whom they supported, the Menzies collectively became one of the largest landholders in the southern Highlands. King James IV created a barony for Sir Robert Menzies, who was probably the original builder of Castle Weem, later called Castle Menzies.

Lands: Atholl, Aberfeldy, Glendochart, Weem.

Associated Castle: Castle Menzies, Perthshire.

MONCREIFFE

Motto: *Sur ésperance* (Upon hope).

Heraldic Badge: A rampant lion issuing from a crest coronet.

Plant: Oak.

Origin of Name: Not many Scottish families have remained in the same home from the beginning of documentary records until now, but the Moncreiffes, whose Gaelic name *Monadh Croibhe* means 'Hill of the Sacred Bough' (i.e. Moncreiffe Hill, near Perth), are one of the exceptions.

Origin of Clan: Descending from the royal Celtic dynasty, the Moncreiffes held great prominence in Scottish and foreign affairs. Sir Mathew of Muncrefe was confirmed in the lands of Moncreiffe in 1248 which were probably inherited.

Lands: Perthshire.

Associated Castle: Tullibole Castle, Perthshire.

MONTGOMERY

Montgomery modern

Motto: *Garde bien (*Watch well).

Heraldic Badge: A woman holds an anchor in her right hand and a bearded head by the hair in her left.

Origin of Name: The name derives from a place in Normandy. Roger de Montgomerie fought for William the Conqueror at the Battle of Hastings. His descendants became lords Montgomery and, in 1507, earls of Eglinton.

Origin of Clan: The first British Montgomery, or Montgomerie, came over with William the Conqueror in 1066 and a (probable) grandson acquired Eaglesham, south of Glasgow, which his family retained until the 19th century. His descendants became lords Montgomery and, in 1507, earls of Eglinton. The 1st Earl held Brodick Castle and the Isle of Arran before the Hamiltons. The Montgomerys were involved in one of Scotland's longest-running feuds, with the Cunninghams.

Lands: Ardrossan, Eglinton, Kintyre.

Associated Castles: Little Cumbrae Castle, North Ayrshire; Eglinton Castle, North Ayrshire; Skelmorlie Castle, Ayrshire.

Morrison ancient

MORRISON

Motto: *Teaghlach Phabbay* (Pabbay Family). Refers to the chief's descent from the Morrisons of Dun Pabbay.

War Cry: *'Dun Uisden'* (Hugh's Castle).

Heraldic Badge: An embattled wall rises from a sea of waves from which extends an arm grasping a dagger.

Plant: Driftwood.

Origin of Name: The name appears in many regions when surnames were coming into fashion, and it is unlikely that the source is the same in all cases. It was most common, however, in the far north-west, and the Morrisons of the Outer Hebrides, who were renowned as poets and musicians, may well have descended from the Irish bards known as O'Muirgheasain.

Origin of Clan: In Lewis, Morrisons held the office of hereditary judge under the MacLeods with land in the district of Ness. They were linked with the Mackenzies in some manner.

Lands: Lewis, Harris, Skye, Sutherland, Aberdeenshire.

Associated Castles: Bognie Castle, Aberdeenshire; Hill Fort of Dùn Èistean, Isle of Lewis.

MUIR

Muir modern

Motto: *Durum patientia frango* (I overcome difficulties by patience).

Heraldic Badge: A bearded head turned in profile to the right.

Origin of Name: The name derives from a word meaning someone who lives beside a moor or heathland, although it is also thought that Muir may derive from the Gaelic for large (*mór*).

Origin of Clan: The Muirs are thought to have descended from the Pictish Celts of both Scotland and Ireland. The clan can trace its ancestry to Ayrshire where the Muirs became prominent figures. When Sir Gilchrist Mure married the daughter and sole heir of Sir Walter Comyn, with the blessing of Alexander III for his part in the battle of Largs, the family's seat was secured at Rowallan Castle. Clan Muir has no chief and is armigerous.

Lands: Ayrshire, Lanarkshire, Berwickshire.

Associated Castle: Rowallan Castle, East Ayrshire.

Munro modern

MUNRO

Motto: Dread God.

War Cry: *'Caisteal Folais 'na Theine'* (Castle Foulis Ablaze).

Heraldic Badge: An eagle rising.

Plant: Common club moss.

Origin of Name: The name is of Gaelic origin meaning 'mouth of the River Rotha' and was given to those who lived near to the river's mouth.

Origin of Clan: The Munros were established in the fertile district north of the Cromarty Firth, becoming the chief residents of Foulis Castle by the 14th century. Their earlier history is uncertain, though one theory traces the name to the River Rotha in Northern Ireland. They were tenants of the earls of Ross, later the Crown, and fought in royal service, with George Munro of Foulis falling in the Battle of Pinkie (1547).

Lands: Easter Ross, lands to the north of the Cromarty Firth.

Associated Castle: Foulis Castle, Highland.

Murray modern

MURRAY

Motto: Furth fortune and fill the fetters.

Heraldic Badge: A naked bearded figure, wreathed about the temples and waist with laurel, his arms extended, holds a dagger in the right hand and a golden key in the left.

Plant: Butcher's broom, juniper.

Origin of Name: The name derives from the place name Moray.

Origin of Clan: Moray was a Pictish kingdom in the early Middle Ages, and the Murrays (or Morays) were no doubt of Pictish descent, though their alleged ancestor, Freskin, may have been a Flemish adventurer. His grandson, William de Moravia, held lands in Moray from David II. He produced many successful offspring, who in turn founded further branches, so that landholding Murrays were to be found all over Scotland in the later Middle Ages.

Lands: Morayshire, Perthshire.

Associated Castles: Bothwell Castle, South Lanarkshire; Balvaird Castle, Perthshire; Blair Castle, Perthshire.

NAPIER

Napier ancient

Motto: *Sans tache* (Without stain).

Heraldic Badge: An extended right arm whose hand grasps a crescent.

Plant: Heather.

Origin of Name: Napier derives from an English word for the person in charge of linen.

Origin of Clan: Family tradition ascribes the origin of the Napiers to the old earls of Lennox, though it is hard to reconcile with the derivation of the word 'naperer'. John de Napier held land of the Earl of Dumbarton in the 13th century and a presumed descendant was governor of Edinburgh Castle in the 14th century. His son, a successful merchant, acquired Merchiston, and many of his successors died fighting for the Crown. John, 8th Laird of Merchiston, was Master of the Mint under James VI. A fierce opponent of Roman Catholicism, he is remembered as the inventor of logarithms.

Lands: Fife, Gosford, Midlothian.

Associated Castles: Napier Merchiston Castle, Edinburgh; Kilmahew Castle, Argyll & Bute.

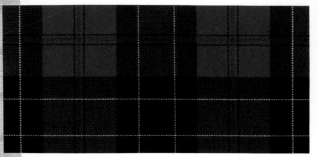

OGILVIE

Motto: *A fin* (To the end).

Heraldic Badge: A woman, cropped at the waist, holds a portcullis.

Plant: Whitethorn, hawthorn.

Origin of Name: The name derives from the lands of Ogilvie, near Glamis in Angus.

Origin of Clan: The presumed founder of the Ogilvies of that ilk was Gillebride, or Gilbert, a son of the Earl (Mormaer) of Angus in the 12th century. He granted the lands of Ogilvie and Easter Powrie to his younger son, also Gilbert, and they were passed down in unbroken male descent for about 500 years. The chiefship, however, belonged to another branch, originally the Ogilvies of Auchterhouse, hereditary sheriffs of Angus in the 14th century. Sir Walter Ogilvie of Auchterhouse was killed at the battle of Harlaw (1411). His younger son was Lord High Treasurer and builder of the Tower of Airlie in 1639 and the acknowledged chief of the clan.

Lands: Angus.

Associated Castle: Airlie Castle, Angus.

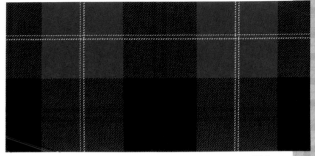

Oliphant modern

OLIPHANT

Motto: *Tout pourvoir* (Provide for all).

Heraldic Badge: A unicorn's head.

Origin of Name: Variants of the name are numerous, and some say the present form resulted from tales of elephants brought back by Crusaders.

Origin of Clan: The Oliphants arrived in England with William the Conqueror in 1066. It is traditionally believed that in 1141, David de Olifard saved David I of Scotland's life in a battle during the English civil war between King Stephen and the Empress Matilda. As a reward, the Olifard family were given lands in Roxburghshire. In 1296, although the Oliphants gave homage to Edward I of England, they backed the Scottish cause in the siege of Edward in 1304 and held Stirling Castle. They gained further territory after victory at the Battle of Bannockburn, when Robert the Bruce granted the Oliphants lands at Gask and Aberdalgie.

Lands: Perthshire.

Associated Castles: Kellie Castle, Fife; Ardblair Castle, Perthshire.

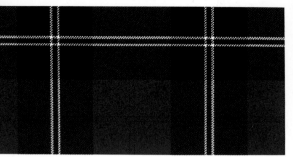

RAMSAY

Ramsey modern

Motto: *Ora et labora* (Pray and work).

Heraldic Badge: A unicorn's head.

Plant: Blue harebell (Scottish bluebell).

Origin of Name: The origin of the name is uncertain, but it was probably a place in Lothian where Simon de Ramsay held land in the 12th century. A presumed descendant held Dalhousie by 1300.

Origin of Clan: The Ramsays of Dalhousie are of Anglo-Norman stock, who prospered and founded several cadet branches. One of these, the Ramsays of Melrose, became earls of Dalhousie in the 17th century. The last of their line was the Marquess of Dalhousie, who became Governor General of India in 1847 at the age of 34.

Lands: Dalhousie, Bamff.

Associated Castles: Dalhousie Castle, Midlothian; Brechin Castle, Angus.

ROBERTSON
OR DONNACHAIDH

Motto: *Virtutis gloria merces* (Glory is the reward).

War Cry: *'Garg 'n uuir dhuis gear'* (Fierce when roused).

Heraldic Badge: A right hand holding aloft an imperial crown.

Plant: Fine-leaved heather, bracken.

Origin of Name: King Duncan's grandson was Robert, from whom most of the clan took their name (others took different names, such as Duncanson). He received the barony of Struan, which is the origin of the name Struan Robertson, by which the chiefs have been known since the 16th century.

Origin of Clan: The Robertsons are *Clann Donnachaidh*, 'children of Duncan'. Duncan was an early 14th-century chief who was himself descended from the old earls of Atholl, and they were descended from King Duncan, who was a son of Abbot Crinan of Dunkeld, guardian of the relics of St. Columba. This inheritance claimed by the Robertsons is no longer disputed.

Lands: Struan.

Associated Castles: Dunalastair Castle, Perthshire; Lude Castle, Perth and Kinross.

Rose modern

ROSE

Motto: Constant and true.

Heraldic Badge: A harp rising from an ermine-trimmed cap.

Plant: Wild rosemary.

Origin of Name: The name is thought to be Norman in origin and derives from Ros.

Origin of Clan: The Roses of Kilravock, near Cawdor, can be traced back to the early 13th century and are thought to be of Norman origin. The chiefs of Rose, generally named Hugh, were lords of Kilravock for about 600 years, succession usually passing from father to son. The family history suggests that it was possible for Highland lairds to live in relative peace with their neighbours. Asked by James VI how he managed it, the 10th Rose of Kilravock, known as the Black Baron, replied that he prayed three times a day instead of once.

Lands: Strathnairn, Ross-shire.

Associated Castle: Kilravock Castle, Highland.

Ross ancient

ROSS

Motto: *Spem successus alit* (Success nourishes hope).

Heraldic Badge: A right hand holds aloft a garland of laurel.

Plant: Juniper.

Origin of Name: The name derives from the place name, Ross-shire.

Origin of Clan: The Rosses claim descent from the old Celtic earls of Ross who, in turn, were probably descended from the Irish High King, Niall of the Nine Hostages. Their homeland was the peninsula of Easter Ross, north of the Cromarty Firth, a fertile land not immediately threatened by land-hungry neighbours. The 4th Earl of Ross married a sister of Robert Bruce and was killed in battle in 1333, even though he was wearing the sacred shirt of St. Duthac, supposed to ensure impregnability. The 5th Earl died without a male heir, which resulted in the conflict over the earldom between the Lord of the Isles and the Regent Albany and the bloody battle of Harlaw (1411).

Lands: Ross-shire, Ayrshire, Renfrewshire.

Associated Castle: Balnagown Castle, Highland.

Ruthven modern

RUTHVEN

Motto: *Deid schaw.*

Heraldic Badge: A ram's head.

Origin of Name: The name derives from the Ruthven lands, north of Loch Rannoch in Perthshire. In Gaelic these lands are called *Ruadhainn.*

Origin of Clan: The clan is thought to be Norse in origin, the founder of the clan having been Thor, son of Sweyn the Viking chief. They first settled in East Lothian, but by the end of the 12th century they had become established in Perthshire. The Ruthvens have a rich history and are known for their dark characters and deeds. The 3rd Lord Ruthven was connected with the murder of David Rizzio, the Italian secretary of Mary, Queen of Scots.

Lands: Perthshire.

Associated Castle: Huntingtower Castle, Perthshire.

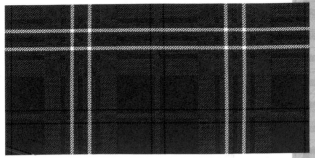

Scott modern

SCOTT

Motto: *Amo* (I love).

War Cry: '*A Bellendaine!*' Also, '*The Scotts are out!*'.

Heraldic Badge: A stag turned to the right.

Plant: Blaeberry.

Origin of Name: The name derives from the Latin word *Scotti*, which was originally used to denote the Irish Celts and later the Gaels.

Origin of Clan: The Scotts can be traced back to the 12th century and the founder of the senior family, the Scotts of Buccleuch, Richard le Scot, whose estates in Lanark where the basis for the considerable holding of his decendants. They acquired Branxholm, still the seat of the dukes of Buccleuch, in the 14th century. As a large Border clan, the Scotts came into their own after the eclipse of the Douglases in 1455.

Lands: Borders, Fife.

Associated Castles: Dalkeith Palace, Midlothian; Bowhill House, Scottish Borders.

SCRYMGEOUR

Scrymgeour ancient

Motto: Dissipate (Disperse).

Heraldic Badge: A lion brandishing a scimitar.

Plant: Rowan.

Origin of Name: The name Scrymgeour is probably derived from *skrymsher*, an old English word for a swordsman.

Origin of Clan: The Scrymgeour family was well-established in Fife long before their connection with Dundee. The Scrymgeours are likely to have descended from the great MacDuff, Earl of Fife. It is belived that when in battle, members of the clan carried the holy pastoral staff of St. Columba.The clan chiefs were later created constables, Earls of Dundee, and hereditary royal standard bearers.

Lands: Fife, Dundee.

Associated Castles: Birkhill Castle, Fife; Dudhope Castle, Dundee; Fincharn Castle, Argyll & Bute.

SETON

Motto: Hazard yet forward.

Heraldic Badge: A green wyvern, spouting fire and with wings extended, rises from a ducal coronet.

Plant: Yew.

Origin of Name: The village of Sai, near Exmes in Normandy, is believed to have given its name to Seton in Scotland by 1150, when Alexander de Seton witnessed a charter by David I of Scotland. This clan has no chief and is armigerous.

Origin of Clan: The Setons were a fortunate clan for they married into the family of Robert the Bruce which led to their security. Later in the 19th century, however, they were less lucky when all the sons were killed in battle, although the family's lands were retained through the female side.

Lands: Lowlands.

Associated Castle: Castle Seton, Later Seton Palace, Midlothian.

Shaw ancient

SHAW

Motto: *Fide et fortitudine* (By fidelity and fortitude).

Heraldic Badge: A right arm with the hand holding a dagger.

Plant: Red whortleberry, boxwood.

Origin of Name: The name Shaw is possibly derived from the Gaelic first name *Sithech*, meaning 'wolf' or 'one who came from a small copse or wood'.

Origin of Clan: The Lowland clan first appears in the 13th century, the name usually appearing around Ayrshire, Kirkcudbrightshire and Stirlingshire. The northern clan was granted lands in Rothiemurchus in 1236 and is descended from Shaw, the son of Gilchrist, grandson of Angus, 6th Chief of Mackintosh.

Lands: Kirkcudbrightshire, Ayrshire, Stirlingshire, Rothiemurchus.

Associated Castle: Doune of Rothiemurchus, Highland.

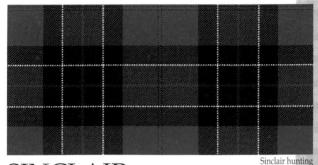

Sinclair hunting

SINCLAIR

Motto: Commit thy work to God.

Heraldic Badge: A cockerel.

Plant: Gorse.

Origin of Name: The name is of Norman origin, and Henry de Saint-Clair held lands in Lothian in the 12th century.

Origin of Clan: The successors of Henry de Saint-Clair became prominent in national affairs: one fought at Bannockburn, another died on Crusade with Douglas in Spain. The son of the latter married the heiress of Orkney and Caithness, and their son became Earl of Orkney, the senior member of the Norwegian nobility, in 1379. He also maintained a considerable fleet engaged in piracy. The Orkney title lasted only two generations after him, but the earldom of Caithness was later restored and is still held.

Lands: Caithness, Midlothian, Orkney.

Associated Castle: Castle Sinclair Girnigoe, Sutherland.

Skene ancient

SKENE

Motto: *Virtutis regia merces* (A palace the reward of bravery).

Heraldic Badge: A right arm extended with the hand holding forth a laurel wreath.

Origin of Name: A 'skene' (*sgian*) is a knife or dagger.

Origin of Clan: The Skenes were a sept of Clan Donnchaidh, most of whom later took the name Robertson, and the barony of Skene, west of Aberdeen, may have been named after its holders rather than, as usual, vice versa. The barony was confirmed by a charter of Bruce in 1318, and the clan, though small, appears to have prospered. Provost Skene's house in Aberdeen, now a museum, was acquired by George Skene in the 17th century. When the last of the lairds of Skene died childless in 1827, the lands passed to a nephew, the Earl of Fife, and the chiefship to an emigrant branch. William Forbes Skene, a great authority on Celtic Scotland in the 19th century, sprang from a cadet branch, the Skenes of Rubislaw.

Lands: Aberdeenshire, Skene.

Associated Castle: Skene Castle, Aberdeenshire.

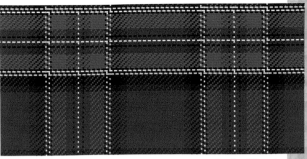

ROYAL STEWART

Royal Stewart modern

Motto: *Virescit vulnere virtus* (Courage grows strong at a wound).

Plant: Thistle.

Origin of Name: Walter FitzAlan, whose ancestors were Bretons rather than Normans (and therefore Celts), came north with David I in 1124. He was appointed to the office of High Steward, which became hereditary in his family and gave it its surname, Stewart.

Origin of Clan: After the Norman conquest the Stewarts acquired estates in England and then Scotland in the reign of David I. The 6th High Steward married Bruce's daughter Marjorie, and when King David II died childless in 1371, their son became the first of the royal dynasty of Robert II, The history of that dynasty is, of course, part of the history not only of Scotland, but also of Great Britain and Ireland. The last of the line was Henry, Cardinal York, brother of Prince Charles Edward ('Bonnie Prince Charlie'), who died in 1788.

Lands: Lauderdale, Renfrewshire, Teviotdale.

Associated Castles: Edinburgh Castle, Stirling Castle, Stirling.

Stewart of Appin modern

STEWART OF APPIN

Motto: *Quhidder will zie* (Whither will ye).

War Cry: *'Creag an Sgairbh'* (The Cormorant's Rock).

Heraldic Badge: A unicorn's head.

Plant: Oak.

Origin of Name: The name derives from the place name 'Appin'.

Origin of Clan: Several notable families, including the Stewarts of Appin who formed a self-contained west Highland clan, traced their descent from Sir James Stewart of Pirston (Pearston), a younger son of the productive Sir John Stewart of Bonkyl. Dugald, the first Stewart of Appin, was five generations removed from Sir James of Pirston and was himself the founder of several cadet branches. Like other Stewarts, the Stewarts of Appin were loyal supporters of their remote royal relations. After taking part in Montrose's campaign of 1645, they signed a bond of association with the Stewarts of Atholl and other branches.

Lands: Appin and Ardshiel.

Associated Castle: Castle Stalker, Argyll.

Sutherland modern

SUTHERLAND

Motto: *Sans peur* (Without fear).

War Cry: *'Ceann na Drochaide Bige'* (The Head of the Little Bridge).

Heraldic Badge: A seated wildcat turned to the right.

Plant: Cotton sedge, butcher's broom.

Origin of Name: The name is Norse, and Sutherland is one of the oldest continuous earldoms in the United Kingdom, created in the early 13th century.

Origin of Clan: The 1st Earl of Sutherland was a descendant of William de Moravia, ancestor of the Murrays, and when surnames came to be generally adopted many Sutherland men took the name Murray. The earls were supporters of Bruce and the 5th Earl's son by a daughter of Bruce might have pre-empted the Stewart succession had he not died young.

Lands: Sutherland.

Associated Castle: Dunrobin Castle, Sutherland.

Thomson modern

THOMSOM
OR MACTHOMAS

Motto: *Deo juvante invidiam superabo* (I will overcome envy with God's help).

Heraldic Badge: A wildcat grasping a serpent in its front right paw, its tail encircling the left.

Plant: Snowberry, red whortleberry.

Origin of Name: This is quite a common name in Scotland, an alternative form of the original Gaelic being MacTavish, the name of a sept of the Campbells of Argyll. Some of them were called Taweson, as well as Thomson, and they may have been related to the Border family Thomson of that ilk.

Origin of Clan: A sept of the MacFarlanes was descended from a younger son of an early MacFarlane chief named Thomas, and a larger group was a sept of Clan Chattan, resident in Glenshee and Glenisla and descended from an illegitimate son of the 7th Mackenzie chief. Their name was most commonly anglicized as MacThomas and the name also appeared in the Isles.

Lands: Glenshee, Glen Prosen, Strathardle.

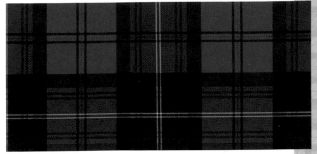

Urquhart modern

URQUHART

Motto: Meane weil, speak weil and doe weil.

War Cry: 'Trust and go forward'.

Heraldic Badge: Rising from a crest coronet, a naked woman holds a sword in her right hand and a palm sapling in her left.

Plant: Wallflower.

Origin of Name: The name appears to derive from a topographical term, but there are several possibilities in Gaelic.

Origin of Clan: Tradition links the Urquharts with Clan Forbes, and at one time they controlled most of the Black Isle. The researches of the scholarly but eccentric Sir Thomas Urquhart of Cromarty (who died in 1660 of joy, it is said, at the Restoration of Charles II) traced Urquhart ancestry to the time of the pyramids, but the first known lived in the 14th century, when the Urquharts gained the office of hereditary sheriffs of Cromarty.

Lands: Ross-shire, Inverness-shire.

Associated Castle: Castle Craig, Highland.

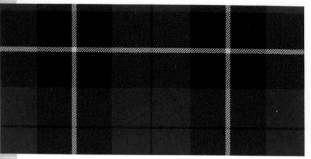

Wallace modern

WALLACE

Motto: *Pro libertate* (For liberty).

War Cry: *'Freedom!'*

Heraldic Badge: An arm clad in armour, the hand holding a sword.

Plant: Oak.

Origin of Name: The name derives from Wallensis meaning 'Welsh'.

Origin of Clan: Richard Wallensis (meaning 'the Welshman', in this case a man of the ancient British kingdom of Strathclyde) was a vassal of Walter the Steward, ancestor of the Stewarts, with land at Richardston (Riccarton), south of Kilmarnock. His grandson, Adam Wallace of Riccarton, had two sons, the younger of whom received lands at Elderslie, near Paisley. There William Wallace, the great national hero, was born in about 1275.

Lands: Ayrshire, Renfrewshire.

Associated Castles: Craigie Castle, South Ayrshire; Auchenbathie Tower, Renfrewshire.

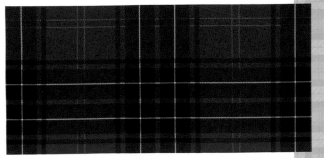

WEMYSS

Motto: *Je pense* (I think).

Heraldic Badge: A swan rising.

Origin of Name: The name may originally have been a corruption of the Gaelic word for 'cave', an interpretation encouraged by the presence of caves, containing Pictish inscriptions, below the ancient ruins of MacDuff's Castle in East Wemyss on the Firth of Forth.

Origin of Clan: The lands of Wemyss, in the Kingdom of Fife, were granted to a younger son of the (MacDuff) Earl of Fife in the early 12th century. There were many branches of the family, but Wemyss of Wemyss was acknowledged as the senior line and the 5th Earl of Wemyss was officially acknowledged as representative of the family of the MacDuff earls of Fife and thus chief of the clan. His son, Lord Elcho, raised troops for Prince Charles Edward in the Forty-Five and died in exile. As a result, the chiefship and the title became permanently separated.

Lands: Fife.

Associated Castles: Castle Wemyss, Fife; Elcho Castle, Perthshire.

SCOTTISH FAMILY NAMES &
THEIR ASSOCIATED CLANS

Abbot	Macnab	Bowie	MacDonald
Abbotson	Macnab	Bowmaker	MacGregor
Addison	Gordon	Bowman	Farquharson
Adie	Gordon	Boyes	Forbes
Aicheson	Gordon	Brebner	Farquharson
Airlie	Ogilvie	Brewer	Drummond,
Aitken	Gordon		MacGregor
Alexander	MacAlister,	Brown	Lamont,
	MacDonald		MacMillan
Alistair	MacAlister	Bryce	MacFarlane
Allan	MacDonald,	Buntain	Graham
	MacFarlane	Bunten	Graham
Allanson	MacDonald,	Buntine	Graham
	MacFarlane	Burdon	Lamont
Allison	MacAlister	Burke	MacDonald
Arrol	Hay	Burnes	Cambell
Arthur	MacArthur	Burns	Cambell
Askey	MacLeod	Cadell	Cambell
Austin	Keith	Caird	Sinclair,
Ayson	Mackintosh		MacGregor
Bain	MacBean,	Cariston	Skene
	MacKay	Carlyle	Bruce
Balloch	MacDonald	Carr	Kerr
Barrie	Farquharson,	Carrick	Kennedy
	Gordon	Carson	MacPherson
Barron	Rose	Cassels	Kennedy
Bartholomew	MacFarlane,	Cattanach	Macpherson
	Leslie	Caw	MacFarlane
Bean	MacBean	Cessford	Kerr
Beath	MacDonald,	Charles	Mackenzie
	MacLean	Christie	Farquharson
Beattie	MacBean	Clanachan	MacLean
Begg	MacDonald	Clark	Cameron,
Berry	Forbes		MacPherson
Beton	MacLeod	Clarke	Cameron,
Binnie	MacBean		MacPherson
Black	Lamont,	Clarkson	Cameron,
	MacGregor,		Macpherson
	MacLean	Clement	Lamont
Blake	Lamont	Clerk	Cameron,
Bonar	Graham		MacPherson
Bontine	Graham	Cluny	MacPherson
Bowers	MacGregor	Clyne	Sinclair

Cobb	Lindsay	Dobson	Robertson
Collier	Robertson	Dochart	MacGregor
Colman	Buchanan	Docharty	MacGregor
Colson	MacDonald	Doig	Drummond
Colyear	Robertson	Doles	Mackintosh
Combie	Thomson	Donachie	Robertson
Comine	Cumming	Donaldson	MacDonald
Comrie	MacGregor	Donillson	MacDonald
Conacher	MacDougall	Donleavy	Buchanan
Connell	MacDonald	Donlevy	Buchanan
Conochie	Campbell	Donnellson	MacDonnell
Constable	Hay	Dove	Buchanan
Cook	Stewart	Dow	Buchanan,
Corbet	Ross		Davidson
Cormack	Buchanan	Dowe	Buchanan
Coull	MacDonald	Downie	Lindsay
Coulson	MacDonald	Drysdale	Douglas
Cousland	Buchanan	Duff	MacDuff
Coutts	Farquharson	Duffus	Sutherland
Cowan	Colquhoun,	Duilach	Stewart
	MacDougall	Duncanson	Robertson
Cowie	Fraser	Dunnachie	Robertson
Crerar	Mackintosh	Duthie	Ross
Crombie	MacDonald	Dyce	Skene
Crookshanks	Stewart	Eadie	Gordon
Cruickshank	Stewart	Eaton	Home
Crum	MacDonald	Edie	Gordon
Cullen	Gordon	Elder	Mackintosh
Cumin	Cumming	Ennis	Innes
Dallas	Mackintosh	Enrick	Gunn
Daniels	MacDonald	Esson	Mackintosh
Davis	Davidson	Ewing	MacLachlan
Dawson	Davidson	Fair	Ross
Day	Davidson	Fairbairn	Armstrong
Dean	Davidson	Federith	Sutherland
Denoon	Campbell	Fergus	Fergusson
Deuchar	Lindsay	Ferries	Fergusson
Dickson	Keith	Ferson	MacPherson
Dingwall	Munro, Ross	Fife	MacDuff
Dinnes	Innes	Findlater	Ogilvie
Dis	Skene	Findlay	Farquharson
Dixon	Keith	Findlayson	Farquharson
Dobbie	Robertson	Finlayson	Farquharson

Fisher	Campbell	Grier	MacGregor
Foulis	Munro	Griesck	MacFarlane
France	Stewart	Grigor	MacGregor
Francis	Stewart	Gruamach	MacFarlane
Frew	Fraser	Gruer	MacGregor,
Frissell	Fraser		Drummond
Frizell	Fraser	Haddon	Graham
Fyfe	MacDuff	Haggart	Ross
Gallie	Gunn	Hallyard	Skene
Galt	MacDonald	Hardie	Farquharson,
Garrow	Stewart		Mackintosh
Garvie	MacLean	Hardy	Farquharson,
Gaunson	Gunn		Mackintosh
Geddes	Gordon	Harold	MacLeod
Georgeson	Gunn	Harper	Buchanan
Gibb	Buchanan	Harperson	Buchanan
Gifford	Hay	Harvey	Keith
Gilbert	Buchanan	Hastings	Campbell
Gilbertson	Buchanan	Hawes	Campbell
Gilbride	MacDonald	Hawson	Campbell
Gilchrist	MacLachlan,	Hawthorn	MacDonald
	Ogilvie	Hendrie	MacNaughton
Gillfillan	MacNab	Hendry	MacNaughton
Gill	MacDonald	Hewitson	MacDonald
Gillanders	Ross	Hewitt	MacDonald
Gillespie	MacPherson	Higginson	Mackintosh
Gillies	MacPherson	Hobson	Robertson
Gillon	MacLean	Hossack	Mackintosh
Gilroy	Grant,	Howe	Graham
	MacGillivray	Howie	Graham
Glennie	Mackintosh	Howison	MacDonald
Gorrie	MacDonald	Hudson	MacDonald
Goudie	MacPherson	Hughson	MacDonald
Gow	MacPherson	Huntly	Gordon
Gowan	MacDonald	Hutchenson	MacDonald
Gowrie	MacDonald	Hutchinson	MacDonald
Greenlaw	Home	Hutchison	MacDonald
Gregorson	MacGregor	Inches	Robertson
Gregory	MacGregor	Ingram	Colquhoun
Greig	MacGregor	Innie	Innes
Greusach	Farquharson	Isles	MacDonald
Grewar	MacGregor,	Jameson	Gunn, Stewart
	Drummond	Jamieson	Gunn, Stewart

Jeffrey	MacDonald	Lombard	Stewart
Kay	Davidson	Lonie	Cameron
Kean	Gunn,	Lorne	Stewart,
	MacDonald		Campbell
Keene	Gunn,	Loudoun	Campbell
	MacDonald	Low	MacLaren
Kellie	MacDonald	Lowson	MacLaren
Kendrick	MacNaughton	Lucas	Lamont
Kenneth	Mackenzie	Luke	Lamont
Kennethson	Mackenzie	Lyall	Sinclair
Kerracher	Farquharson	Maca'challies	MacDonald
Kilgour	MacDuff	Macachounich	Colquhoun
King	Colquhoun	MacAdam	MacGregor
Kinnell	MacDonald	MacAdie	Fergusson
Kinnieson	MacFarlane	MacAindra	MacFarlane
Knox	MacFarlane	MacAldonich	Buchanan
Lachie	MacLachlan	MacAlduie	Lamont
Laidlaw	Scott	MacAllan	MacDonald,
Lair	MacLaren		MacFarlane
Lamb	Lamont	MacAlonie	Cameron
Lambie	Lamont	MacAndeoir	Buchanan,
Lammond	Lamont		MacNab
Lamondson	Lamont	MacAndrew	Mackintosh
Landers	Lamont	MacAngus	MacInnes
Lang	Leslie	MacAra	MacGregor,
Lansdale	Home		MacRae
Lauchlan	MacLauchlan	MacArec	MacGregor
Lawrence	MacLaren	MacAskill	MacLeod
Lawrie	MacLaren	MacAslan	Buchanan
Lawson	MacLaren	MacAuselan	Buchanan
Lean	MacLean	MacAusland	Buchanan
Leckie	MacGregor	MacAuslane	Buchanan
Lecky	MacGregor	MacBaxter	MacMillan,
Lees	MacPherson		MacDonald,
Leitch	MacDonald		MacLean
Lemond	Lamont	MacBeolain	MacKenzie
Lennie	Buchanan	MacBeth	MacBean,
Lewis	MacLeod		MacDonald,
Limond	Lamont		MacLean
Limont	Lamont	MacBheath	MacBean,
Linklater	Sinclair		MacDonald,
Lobban	Logan		MacLean
Lockerbie	Douglas	MacBride	MacDonald

MacBrieve	Morrison	MacConchy	Mackintosh
MacBurie	MacDonald	MacCondy	MacFarlane
MacCaa	MacFarlane	MacConnach	Mackenzie
MacCabe	MacLeod	MacConnechy	Campbell,
MacCaig	Farquharson,		Robertson
	MacLeod	MacConnell	MacDonald
MacCall	MacDonald	MacCooish	MacDonald
MacCalman	Buchanan	MacCorkhill	Gunn
MacCalmont	Buchanan	MacCorkindale	MacLeod
MacCamie	Stewart	MacCorkle	Gunn
MacCammon	Buchanan	MacCormack	Buchanan
MacCammond	Buchanan	MacCormick	MacLaine of
MacCanish	MacInness		Lochbuie
MacCartney	Farquharson,	MacCorrie	MacQuarrie
	Mackintosh	MacCorry	MacQuarrie
MacCartair	Campbell	MacCosram	MacDonald
MacCarter	Campbell	MacCoull	MacDougall
MacCash	MacDonald	MacCowan	Colquhoun,
MacCaskill	MacLeod		MacDougall
MacCasland	Buchanan	MacCrae	MacRae
MacCaul	MacDonald	MacCrain	MacDonald
MacCause	MacFarlane	MacCraken	MacLean
MacCaw	MacFarlane	MacCraw	MacRae
MacCay	MacKay	MacCreath	MacRae
MacCeallaich	MacDonald	MacCrie	MacKay
MacChlerich	Cameron	MacCrimmor	MacLeod
MacChlery	Cameron	MacCrindle	MacDonald
MacChoiter	MacGregor	MacCririe	MacDonald
MacChruiter	Buchanan	MacCrouther	MacGregor,
MacCloy	Stewart		Drummond
MacClure	MacLeod	MacCruithein	MacDonald
MacCluskie	MacDonald	MacCuag	MacDonald
MacClymont	Lamont	MacCuaig	Farquharson,
MacCodrum	MacDonald		MacLeod
MacColl	MacDonald	MacCubbin	Buchanan
MacColman	Buchanan	MacCuish	MacDonald
MacComas	Thomson	MacCune	MacEwan
MacCombe	Thomson	MacCunn	MacPherson
MacCombich	Stewart of Appin	MacCurrach	MacPherson
MacCombie	Thomson	MacCutchen	MacDonald
MacConacher	MacDougall	MacCutcheon	MacDonald
MacConachie	MacGregor,	MacDade	Davidson
	Robertson	MacDaid	Davidson

MacDaniell	MacDonald	MacGilvernock	Graham
MacDavid	Davidson	MacGilvra	MacGillivray
MacDermid	Campbell	MacGorrie	MacDonald
MacDonachie	Robertson	MacGorry	MacDonald
MacDonleavy	Buchanan	MacGoun	MacDonald,
MacDrain	MacDonald		MacPherson
MacDulothe	MacDougall	MacGowan	MacDonald,
MacEachan	MacDonald of		MacPherson
	Clanranald	MacGown	MacDonald,
MacEachern	MacDonald		MacPherson
MacEaracher	Farquharson	MacGrath	MacRae
MacElfrish	MacDonald	MacGreusich	Buchanan,
MacElheran	MacDonald		MacFarlane
MacEoin	MacFarlane	MacGrewar	MacGregor,
MacEol	MacNaughton		Drummond
MacErracher	MacFarlane	MacGrime	Graham
MacFadzean	MacLaine of	MacGrory	MacLaren
	Lochburie	MacGrowther	MacGregor,
MacFall	MacPherson		Drummond
MacFarquhar	Farquharson	MacGuaran	MacQuarrie
MacFater	MacLaren	MacGugan	MacNeil
MacFeat	MacLaren	MacGuire	MacQuarrie
MacFergus	Fergusson	Machardie	Farquharson,
MacGaw	MacFarlane		Mackintosh
MacGeachie	MacDonald of	MacHardy	Farquharson,
	Clanranald		Mackintosh
MacGeachin	MacDonald of	MacHarold	MacLeod
	Clanranald	MacHendrie	MacNaughton
MacGeoch	MacFarlane	MacHendry	MacNaughton,
MacGhee	MacKay		MacDonald
MacGhie	MacKay	MacHowell	MacDouglall
MacGilbert	Buchanan	MacHugh	MacDonald
MacGilchrist	MacLachlan,	MacHutchen	MacDonald
	Ogilvie	MacIan	Gunn,
MacGill	MacDonald		MacDonald
MacGilledon	Lamont	MacIldowie	Cameron
MacGillegowie	Lamont	MacIlduy	MacGregor,
MacGillivantic	MacDonald		MacLean
MacGillivour	MacGillivray	MacIlreach	MacDonald
MacGillonie	Cameron	MacIlleriach	MacDonald
MacGilp	MacDonald	Macilriache	MacDonald
MacGilroy	Grant,	MacIlrevie	MacDonald
	MacGillivray	MacIlvain	MacBean

MacIlvora	MacLaine of Lochbuie	MacKichan	MacDonald of Clanranald, MacDougall
MacIlvrae	MacGillivray		
MacIlvride	MacDonald	MacKieson	Mackintosh
MacIlwhom	Lamont	MacKiggan	MacDonald
MacIlwraith	MacDonald	MacKilligan	Mackintosh
MacIlzegowie	Lamont	MacKillop	MacDonald
MacImmey	Fraser	MacKim	Fraser
MacInally	Buchanan	MacKimmie	Fraser
MacInroy	Robertson	MacKindlay	Farquharson
MacInstalker	MacFarlane	MacKinlay	Buchanan, Farquharson, Stewart of Appin
MacIock	MacFarlane		
MacIssac	Campbell, MacDonald		
		MacKinley	Buchanan
MacJames	MacFarlane	MacKinnell	MacDonald
MacKail	Cameron	MacKinney	MacKinnon
MacKames	Gunn	MacKinning	MacKinnon
MacKaskill	MacLeod	MacKinven	MacKinnon
MacKeachan	MacDonald	MacKirdy	Stewart
MacKeamish	Gunn, MacDonald	MacKissock	Campbell, MacDonald of Clanranald
MacKechnie	MacDonald of Clanranald		
		MacKnight	MacNaughton
MacKee	MacKay	MacLae	Stewart of Appin
MacKeggie	Mackintosh	MacLagan	Robertson
MacKeith	MacPherson	MacLaghlan	MacLachlan
MacKellachie	MacDonald	MacLairish	MacDonald
Mackellaigh	MacDonald	MacLamond	Lamont
MacKellar	Campbell	MacLardie	MacDonald
MacKelloch	MacDonald	MacLardy	MacDonald
MacKelvie	Campbell	MacLarty	MacDonald
MacKendrick	MacNaughton	MacLaverty	MacDonald
MacKenrick	MacNaughton	MacLaws	Campbell
MacKeochan	MacDonald of Clanranald	MacLea	Stewart of Appin
		MacLeay	Stewart of Appin
MacKerchar	Farquharson	MacLehose	Campbell
MacKerlich	Mackenzie	MacLeish	MacPherson
MacKerracher	Farquharson	MacLeister	MacGregor
MacKerras	Fergusson	MacLergain	MacLean
MacKersey	Fergusson	MacLerie	Cameron, Mackintosh, MacPherson
MacKessock	Campbell, MacDonald of Clanranald		
		MacLeverty	MacDonald

MacLewis	MacLeod	MacNeish	MacGregor
MacLintock	MacDougall	MacNeur	MacFarlane
MacLise	MacPherson	MacNey	MacGregor
MacLiver	MacGregor	MacNider	MacFarlane
MacLucas	Lamont,	MacNie	MacGregor
	MacDougall	MacNish	MacGregor
MacLugash	MacDougall	MacNiter	MacFarlane
MacLulich	MacDougall,	MacNiven	Cumming,
	Munro, Ross		MacKintosh,
MacLure	MacLeod		MacNaughton
MacLymont	Lamont	MacNuir	MacNaughton
MacManus	Colquhoun,	MacNuyer	Buchanan,
	Gunn		MacNaughton
MacMartin	Cameron	MacOmie	Thomson
MacMaster	Buchanan,	MacOmish	Thomson
	MacInnes	MacOnie	Cameron
MacMath	Matheson	MacOran	Campbell
MacMaurice	Buchanan	MacO'Shannaig	MacDonald
MacMenzies	Menzies	MacOwl	MacDougall
MacMichael	Stewart of Appin	MacPatrick	Lamont,
MacMinn	Menzies		MacLaren
MacMonies	Menzies	MacPetrie	MacGregor
MacMorran	MacKinnon	MacPhadden	MacLaine of
MacMunn	Stewart		Lochbuie
MacMurchie	Buchanan,	MacPhater	MacLaren
	MacKenzie	MacPhedran	Campbell
MacMurchy	Buchanan,	MacPhedron	MacAulay
	Mackenzie	MacPheidiran	MacAulay
MacMurdo	MacPherson	MacPhillip	MacDonald
MacMurdoch	MacPherson	MacPhorich	Lamont
MacMurray	Murray	MacPhun	Matheson,
MacMurrich	MacDonald of		Campbell
	Clanranald,		
	MacPherson	MacQuaire	MacQuarrie
MacMutrie	Stewart	MacQuey	MacKay
MacNair	MacFarlane,	MacQuhirr	MacQuarrie
	MacNaughton	MacQuistan	MacDonald
		MacQuire	MacQuarrie
MacNamell	MacDouglal	MacQuoid	MacKay
MacNayer	MacNaughton	MacRa	MacRae
MacNee	MacGregor	MacRach	MacRae
MacNeilage	MacNeil	MacRaild	MacLeod
MacNeiledge	MacNeil	MacRaith	MacRae,
MacNeilly	MacNeil		MacDonald

MacRankin	MacLean	MacVurie	MacDonald of
MacRath	MacRae		Clanranald
MacRob	Gunn,	MacWalrich	Cameron
	MacFarlane	MacWalter	MacFarlane
MacRobbie	Robertson,	MacWattie	Buchanan
	Drummond	MacWhannell	MacDonald
MacRobert	Robertson,	MacWhirr	MacQuarrie
	Drummond	MacWhirter	Buchanan
MacRorie	MacDonald	MacWilliam	Gunn,
MacRory	MacDonald		MacFarlane
MacRuer	MacDonald		
MacRurie	MacDonald	Malcolmson	MacCallum
MacRury	MacDonald	Malloch	MacGregor
MacShannachan	MacDonald	Mann	Gunn
MacShimes	Fraser of Lovat	Manson	Gunn
MacSorley	Cameron,	Mark	MacDonald
	MacDonald	Marnoch	Innes
MacSporran	MacDonald	Marshall	Keith
MacSwan	MacDonald	Martin	Cameron,
MacSween	MacDonald		MacDonald
MacSwen	MacDonald	Mason	Sinclair
MacSymon	Fraser	Massey	Matheson
MacTaggart	Ross	Masterson	Buchanan
MacTary	Innes	Mathie	Matheson
MacTause	Campbell	Mavor	Gordon
MacTavish	Campbell	May	MacDonald
MacTear	Ross, MacIntyre	Means	Menzies
MacTier	Ross	Meilkeham	Lamont
MacTire	Ross	Mein	Menzies
MacUlric	Cameron	Mennie	Menzies
MacUre	Campbell	Meyners	Menzies
MacVail	Cameron,	Michie	Forbes
	MacKay	Miller	MacFarlane
MacVanish	Mackenzie	Milne	Gordon, Ogilvie
MacVarish	MacDonald of	Milroy	MacGillivrary
	Clanranald	Minn	Menzies
MacVeagh	MacLean	Minnus	Menzies
MacVey	MacBean	Mitchell	Innes
MacVicar	MacNaughton	Monach	MacFarlane
MacVinish	Mackenzie	Monzie	Menzies
MacVurich	MacDonald of	Moodie	Stewart
	Clanranald,	Moray	Murray
	MacPherson	Morgan	MacKay
		Morren	MacKinnon

Simpson	Fraser of Lovat	Walters	Forbes
Simson	Fraser of Lovat	Wass	Monro, Ross
Skinner	MacGregor	Watt	Buchanan
Small	Murray	Weaver	MacFarlane
Smart	Mackenzie	Webster	MacFarlane
Smith	MacPherson,	Whannell	MacDonald
	Mackintosh	Wharrie	MacQuarrie
Sorely	Cameron,	Wheelan	MacDonald,
	MacDonald		MacGregor
Spence	MacDuff	White	MacGregor,
Spittal	Buchanan		Lamont
Spittel	Buchanan	Whyte	MacGregor,
Sporran	MacDonald		Lamont
Stalker	MacFarlane	Wilkie	MacDonald
Stark	Robertson	Wilkinson	MacDonald
Stenhouse	Bruce	Will	Gunn
Storie	Olgilvie	Williamson	Gunn, MacKay
Stringer	MacGregor	Wilson	Gunn, Innes
Summers	Lindsay	Wright	MacIntyre
Suttie	Grant	Wylie	Gunn,
Swan	Gunn		MacFarlane
Swanson	Gunn	Yuill	Buchanan
Syme	Fraser	Yule	Buchanan
Symon	Fraser		
Taggart	Ross		
Tarrill	Mackintosh		
Tawesson	Campbell		
Tawse	Farquharson		
Thain	Innes,		
	Mackintosh		
Todd	Gordon		
Tolmie	MacLeod		
Tonnochy	Robertson		
Torry	Campbell		
Tosh	Mackintosh		
Toward	Lamont		
Towart	Lamont		
Train	Ross		
Turner	Lamont		
Tyre	MacIntyre		
Ure	Campbell		
Vass	Monro, Ross		
Wallis	Wallace		

THE KINGS & QUEENS OF SCOTLAND (FROM 843 TO THE ACT OF UNION 1707)

Kenneth I (MacAlpin) 843–860

Donald I 860–863

Constantine I 863–877

Aodh 877–878

Eocha 878–889

Donald II 889–900

Constantine II 900–943

Malcolm I 943–954

Indulph 954–962

Dubh 962–967

Culiean 967–971

Kenneth II 971–995

Constantine III 995–997

Kenneth III 997–1005

Malcolm II 1005–1034

Duncan I 1034–1040

MacBeth 1040–1057

Lulech 1057 (slain)

Malcolm III (Canmore) 1057–1093

Donald Ban 1093 (deposed)

Duncan II 1094 (slain)

Donald Ban (restored) 1094–1097

Edgar 1097–1107

Alexander I 1107–1124

David I 1124–1153

Malcolm IV (The Maiden) 1153–1165

William I (The Lion) 1165–1214

Alexander II 1214–1249

Alexander III 1249–1286

Margaret (Maid of Norway) 1286–1290

First Interregnum 1290–1292

John Balliol 1292–1296

Second Interregnum 1296–1306

Robert I (the Bruce) 1306–1329

David II 1329–1371

Robert II (Stewart) 1371–1390

Robert III 1390–1406

James I 1406–1437

James II 1437–1460

James III 1460–1488

James IV 1488–1513

James V 1513–1542

Mary, Queen of Scots 1542–1567

James VI 1567–1625

Charles I 1625-1649

The Commonwealth & Protectorate 1651–1660

Charles I 1660–1665 (crowned 1651, exiled and restored 1660)

James VII 1685–1688

Mary II (with William II) 1689–1694

William II 1689–1702

Anne 1702–1714

ACKNOWLEDGEMENTS

© Shutterstock.com. Pages 2, 3, 5, 6, 7, 8, 9, 10, 11, 12, 13, 14, 15, 16, 17, 19, 20, 22, 23, 24, 25, 26, 28, 30, 31, 126.

Wikimedia commons/celtus. Pages 18, 27, 29, 32, 33, 34, 36, 38, 39, 42, 43, 44, 45, 46, 47, 48, 50, 52, 55, 56, 57, 58, 59, 60, 61, 63, 64, 70, 75, 76, 78, 80, 82, 83, 84, 85, 86, 87, 89, 90, 91, 93, 96, 97, 98, 99, 103, 104, 105, 106, 108, 109, 110, 112,113, 114, 115, 116, 118, 119, 121, 123, 124, 127, 129, 130, 131.

Regency House Publishing Ltd. © Pages 21, 35, 37, 40, 41, 44, 49, 51, 53, 54, 62, 65, 66, 67, 68, 69, 71, 73, 73, 74 77, 79, 81, 88, 92, 94, 95, 100, 101, 102, 107, 111, 117, 120, 122, 126, 128.

The publisher would like to thank Paul Manley for his help.